AN INVESTIGATION OF ETHNOGRAPHIC AND ARCHAEOLOGICAL SPECIMENS OF

MESCALBEANS *(SOPHORA SECUNDIFLORA)* IN AMERICAN MUSEUMS

MUSEUM OF ANTHROPOLOGY, THE UNIVERSITY OF MICHIGAN

TECHNICAL REPORTS

Number 6

RESEARCH REPORTS IN ETHNOBOTANY

Contribution 1

AN INVESTIGATION OF ETHNOGRAPHIC AND ARCHAEOLOGICAL SPECIMENS OF MESCALBEANS *(SOPHORA SECUNDIFLORA)* IN AMERICAN MUSEUMS

by

William L. Merrill

ANN ARBOR

1977

Figure 1, Frontispiece. A-se-permy or John White Man, a Comanche, wearing crossed mescalbean bandoleers and single mescalbeans strung onto the shoulder fringe of his shirt. Photograph taken by H. P. Robinson at Fort Sill, Oklahoma Territory, prior to 1895. Reproduced courtesy of the National Anthropological Archives, Smithsonian Institution (negative number 42998-B).

© 1977 Regents of The University of Michigan
The Museum of Anthropology
All rights reserved

Printed in the
United States of America

CONTENTS

		Page
List of Illustrations		vii
List of Tables		viii
Preface		ix
Acknowledgements		xi

I.   Introduction 1
       Botany, Chemistry, and Pharmacology of Mescalbeans . . . 1
       The Use of Mescalbeans in Aboriginal North America . . . 5

II. Mescalbeans in North American Indian Material Culture. . . 16
       Some Qualifications. 17
       Mescalbeans and Material Culture 19

III. Some Ethnographic Problems 27
       The Distribution of the Use of Mescalbeans Among
       Historic North American Indian Groups. 28
       Mescalbeans and Coralbeans 35
       Cross-Cultural Variation in the Use of Mescalbeans . . . 43
       Mescalbeans and Peyote 51

IV. Description of Specimens 63
       Archaeological Specimens 65
           Prehistoric Southwestern Texas 68
       Ethnographic Specimens 70
           Apache 70
           Arapaho. 73
           Arikara. 81
           Blackfoot. 81
           Caddo. 81
           Cheyenne 82
           Coahuilteco. 93
           Comanche 94
           Crow 99
           Delaware 99
           Hidatsa. 100
           Iowa 100
           Kansa. 104
           Kickapoo 105
           Kiowa. 105
           Kiowa-Apache 118

	Page
Mandan	118
Missouri	118
Ojibwa	119
Omaha	119
Osage	122
Oto	123
Pawnee	126
Ponca	129
Prairie Potawatomi	131
Pueblos	134
Sac and Fox	134
Shawnee	138
Shoshone and Northern Ute	138
Sioux	144
Tonkawa	150
Wichita	152
Winnebago	154
Unidentified	155
Appendix I. Index of Specimens by Museum	157
Literature Cited	159

ILLUSTRATIONS

		Page
1.	A-se-permy or John White Man, a Comanche.	ii
2.	Comparison of Sophora secundiflora and Erythrina flabelliformis.	2
3.	The natural ranges of Sophora secundiflora and Erythrina flabelliformis.	3
4.	Approximate locations of Indian groups discussed in text	6
5a.	Prehistoric loincloth bearing mescalbeans	66
5b.	Enlarged view of the same specimen.	67
6.	Prehistoric "medicine bundle" containing mescalbeans.	69
7a.	Arapaho leggings.	74
7b.	Enlarged view of the same specimen.	75
8.	Mescalbeans and coralbeans on an Arapaho shirt.	76
9.	Cheyenne hair ornament.	84
10.	Northern Cheyenne rawhide bag	90
11.	Northern Cheyenne mescalbean necklace or bandoleer.	91
12.	Northern Cheyenne woman's "sack of medicine"	92
13.	Iowa Red Bean medicine bundle	103
14.	Two Kiowa individuals wearing mescalbeans	107
15.	Kiowa mescalbean necklace	112
16.	Kiowa "male warrior doll"	114
17.	Setûñtekûñ or War Bonnet, a Kiowa-Apache.	117
18.	Omaha girl's hair ornament.	120
19.	Pawnee snapping turtle paw bag.	128
20.	Mescalbeans at Taos Pueblo.	132
21a.	Shoshone shirt.	139
21b.	Enlarged view of the same specimen.	140
22.	Brule man wearing a mescalbean hair ornament.	143
23a.	Sioux bearclaw necklace	146
23b.	Enlarged view of the same specimen.	147
24.	Wichita leggings.	151

TABLES

		Pages
1.	Categories of items associated with mescalbeans by group.	32-33
2.	The association of Sophora secundiflora and Erythrina flabelliformis on particular items of material culture by group.	38-40
3.	Age and sex of mescalbean users by group.	45-46

PREFACE

Mescalbeans have attracted the attention of the academic community primarily because several North American Indian groups consumed these seeds for their psychotropic effects. The exploitation of the psychotropic properties of mescalbeans was the most dramatic use of mescalbeans by North American Indian groups, and the most elaborate symbolism and ceremonialism associated with the use of mescalbeans was developed by those American Indian groups who employed them in this fashion. Yet, of the more than thirty North American Indian groups who were familiar with mescalbeans, less than half are known ever to have consumed them. Without question, the most widespread and continuous purpose for which North American Indian groups have employed mescalbeans is as seed beads attached to a wide variety of articles such as shirts, leggings, dresses, and pouches or strung into bandoleers, necklaces, and bracelets. Most if not all ethnographically documented North American Indian groups who had access to mescalbeans utilized them as seed beads, and many of these groups employed mescalbeans for no other purposes. In addition, archaeological evidence indicates that at least some of the Archaic inhabitants of southwestern Texas attached mescalbeans to their clothing during prehistoric times.

In this report, I do not intend to disparage the importance of mescalbeans as a psychotropic substance. Mescalbeans were one of very few plant materials whose psychotropic properties were exploited by the

Indians of North America prior to their placement on reservations and the subsequent widespread diffusion of the peyote cactus. However, most writers who have discussed the North American Indians' use of mescalbeans have stressed the importance of these seeds as a psychotropic substance while almost entirely overlooking their less dramatic role as seed beads. By emphasizing the importance of mescalbeans in North American Indian <u>material</u> culture, I hope to place the use of mescalbeans in aboriginal North America into what I consider its proper perspective.

This report is not designed to be a traditional material culture study that concentrates on such things as manufacturing techniques or nuances of style. Instead, the data collected on the use of mescalbeans in the material culture of a number of North American Indian groups are intended to assist in solving several ethnographic problems that are not particularly materialistic in nature. Nonetheless, I will briefly discuss the manner in which various North American Indian groups have employed mescalbeans as items of material culture, and I will provide descriptions of the archaeological and ethnographic specimens of mescalbeans for which I have information. In fact, I have described the specimens in what some readers will feel is excruciating detail, but I hope these detailed descriptions will allow readers to determine for themselves if my interpretations of the data are valid and will save future investigators the time and energy of having to duplicate my efforts. I also hope that this study will stimulate others to turn to museum collections for the information they need to solve ethnographic problems for which the published literature has not provided and perhaps cannot provide answers.

ACKNOWLEDGEMENTS

This study was motivated by my desire to secure data that would serve to supplement and illuminate the relatively meager published information on the use of mescalbeans by the Indians of North America. I am indebted to Professor Volney H. Jones of the University of Michigan for suggesting that the kind of information I was seeking might be located in the storage rooms and archives of American museums. Professor Jones began collecting notes on the use of mescalbeans by the Indians of North America in 1932, and he examined his first museum specimens of mescalbeans the following year. During the more than forty subsequent years, he has examined a considerable number of additional museum specimens of mescalbeans and amassed an extensive collection of notes on mescalbeans gleaned from widely scattered published and unpublished sources. In 1973, Professor Jones made his entire collection of mescalbean notes available to me, noting that his examination of museum collections of mescalbeans had been rather ad hoc. The number and diversity of sources represented in Professor Jones' notes suggested that little additional information on the use of mescalbeans by the Indians of North America could be rooted out of the existing ethnographic literature. On the other hand, the fact that he encountered a number of ethnographic specimens of mescalbeans while for the most part simply touring museum exhibits seemed to indicate that a systematic examination of museum collections of American Indian materials would reveal an even larger number of specimens of mescalbeans and produce previously unavailable information on the North American Indians' use of mescalbeans. In anticipation of locating such untapped sources of information, the present study was initiated.

During July 1975, I examined specimens of mescalbeans in the collections of the following institutions: Dayton Museum of Natural History, Smithsonian Institution, University Museum (University of Pennsylvania), American Museum of Natural History, Museum of the American Indian (Heye Foundation), Peabody Museum of Natural History (Yale University), and Peabody Museum of Archaeology and Ethnology (Harvard University). During this same period, I consulted archival materials in the National Anthropological Archives (Smithsonian Institution), the Department of Anthropology of the American Museum of Natural History, the Beinecke Rare Book and Manuscript Library (Yale University), and the Libraries of the Gray Herbarium and Arnold Arboretum (Harvard University). Both preceding and following my visits to these museums and archives, I secured through correspondence descriptions of additional specimens of mescalbeans from the Academy of Natural Sciences of Philadelphia, the Arizona State Museum (University of Arizona), the Denver Art Museum, the Lowie Museum of Anthropology (University of California at Berkeley), the Museum of the Plains Indian, the State Historical Society of Wisconsin, the Museum of Texas Tech University, and the Texas Archeological Research Laboratory (University of Texas at Austin).

This research was supported by funds received from the Wenner-Gren Foundation for Anthropological Research, Inc. (Grant # 3074) and the

Phillips Fund of the American Philosophical Society. I am grateful to these foundations for the financial support they so graciously provided and to the directors and staff of the institutions listed above for making this research both possible and enjoyable. In addition, I would like to express my appreciation to Mary Hodge for her careful editing of the manuscript, to Jane Mariouw for drawing the maps and the botanical illustration, and to other members of the technical staff of the Museum of Anthropology, University of Michigan, for their assistance in the preparation of the report.

Finally, I would like to thank three individuals who, through their generous contributions of time and knowledge, greatly assisted me in the completion of this research project. Richard I. Ford first suggested that I undertake the project and provided invaluable guidance and encouragement during its completion. Cecilia Troop Merrill willingly joined me in the exhausting and often frustrating search through museum collections and suggested insightful interpretations of the material we discovered, interpretations that I otherwise would not have considered. Volney H. Jones, by generously allowing me free access to his copious notes and discussing at length my interpretations of them, saved me considerable research time. This project and the results reported herein should be considered a continuation and in some respects a culmination of a portion of the research begun by Professor Jones in 1932.

I. INTRODUCTION

BOTANY, CHEMISTRY, AND PHARMACOLOGY OF MESCALBEANS

Mescalbeans are the seeds of the evergreen shrub or small tree Sophora secundiflora (Ortega) Lagasca ex de Candolle, a member of the Leguminosae (Fabaceae) family (see Fig. 2). The S. secundiflora plant bears its seeds in woody, indehiscent pods, which contain from one to eight seeds and often remain on the plant for several seasons after they first appear. Mescalbeans range in size from 0.8 to 2.0 cm long and from 0.5 to 1.5 cm broad. They usually are ovoid in shape. The seeds display a rather distinctive hilum, or seed scar, which is deeply impressed and usually a different color than the remainder of the seed. Mescalbeans normally vary from maroon to orange-red in color, though yellow ones also occur. Plants bearing yellow mescalbeans have been assigned to a distinct taxonomic category--S. secundiflora forma xanthosperma Rehder--and to date are known to have been collected only in Texas (Rudd 1968:528-30). Sophora secundiflora reaches the northern limits of its natural distribution in southeastern New Mexico and central Texas, and its range extends on the eastern side of the Sierra Madre Occidental as far south as the Mexican states of Puebla and Oaxaca (see Fig. 3).

The physiological effects following the human consumption of mescalbeans reportedly range from nausea and headache to death and include emesis, evacuation of the bowels, the phenomenon of seeing red, cramps

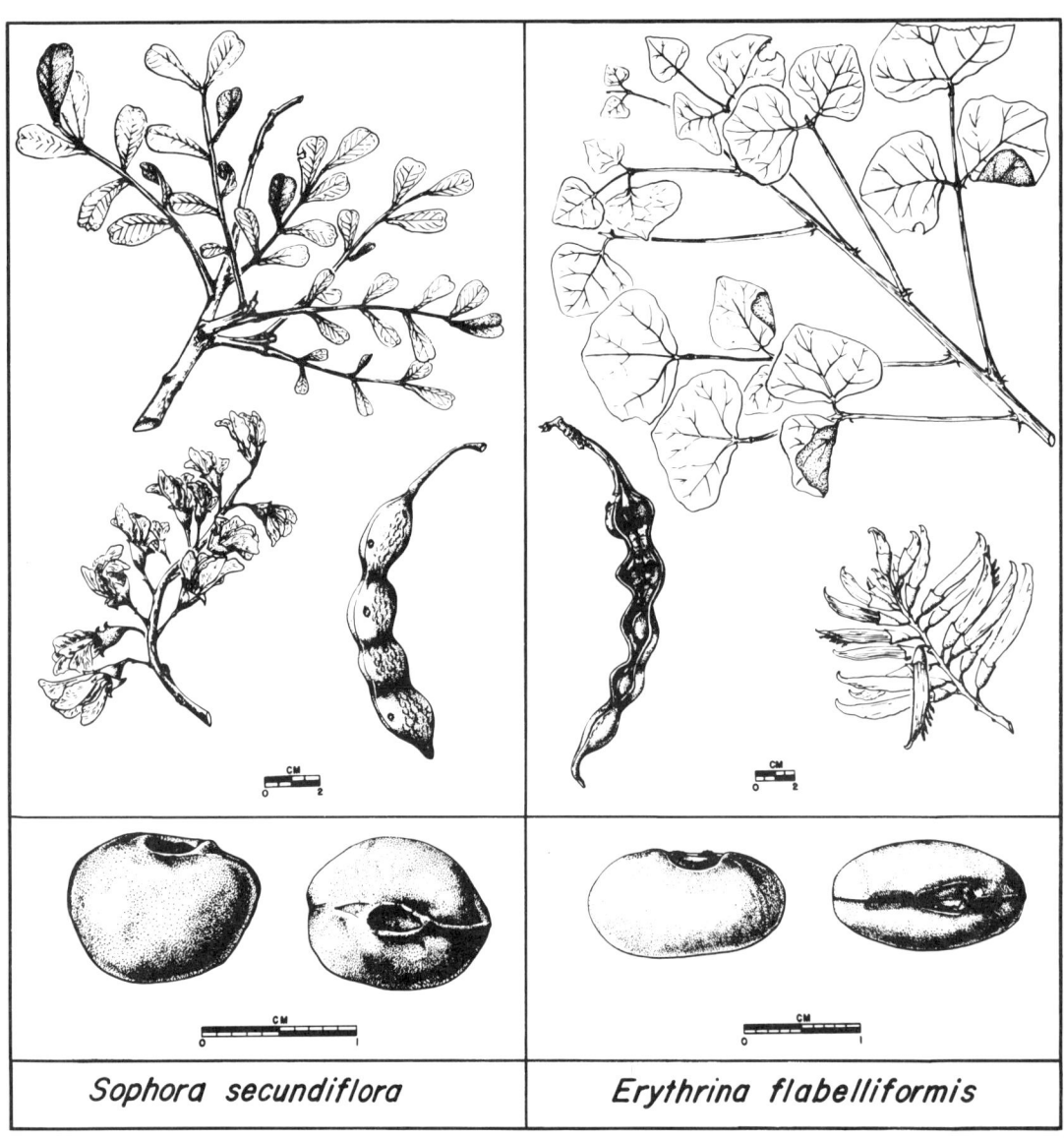

Figure 2. A comparison of Sophora secundiflora and Erythrina flabelliformis.

Figure 3. The natural ranges of <u>Sophora secundiflora</u> and <u>Erythrina flabelliformis</u> (after Jones and Merrill n.d.: Fig. 3; Hastings, et al. 1972:102-232).

in the arms and legs, muscle paralysis, intoxication, insensitivity to pain, stupor, and unconsciousness. The nature of the effects and their intensity and duration appear to be dependent primarily upon the number of mescalbeans consumed, though the manner in which the seeds are prepared for consumption may influence subsequent pharmacologic activity (Jones and Merrill n.d.). The principal alkaloids present in mescalbeans which are believed to be at least partially responsible for these effects are cytisine, N-methylcytisine, and sparteine, all closely related members of the quinolizidine (or lupine) group of alkaloids (Hatfield et al., n.d.).

Although several North American Indian groups associated their consumption of mescalbeans with the receipt of visions, there is no evidence that any of these alkaloids, ingested either in isolation or in combination with the others, are capable of inducing hallucinations. The available ethnographic evidence seems to indicate that the North American Indian groups who employed mescalbeans in their quest for visions did so with the intention of inducing in the individual vision-seeker the physiological state culturally defined as appropriate to the receipt of visions. Such states were achieved in other contexts and by other groups through alternative means such as self-deprivation and meditation. It is unlikely that the consumption of mescalbeans alone was directly or solely responsible for any reported visionary experiences. Rather, the visions seem to have resulted from the combined impact of several factors, including the physiological effects of the mescalbean alkaloids, the dramatic and frequently intense sensory stimulation characteristic of the ceremonial contexts in which mescalbeans were consumed, and the vision-seeker's belief and expectation that visions were both possible and likely to occur in such contexts (Hatfield et al., n.d.).

THE USE OF MESCALBEANS IN ABORIGINAL NORTH AMERICA

Much of the available archaeological and ethnographic evidence for the use of mescalbeans in native North America has been presented and discussed extensively in summary articles by Campbell (1958), Howard (1957), Troike (1962), and Jones and Merrill (n.d.). Since only a general recapitulation of this evidence is presented here, the interested reader is directed to these articles for more detailed accounts of the data upon which this overview is based. In this chapter and in Chapters 2 and 3, I have indicated the original sources of my information only when those sources are not noted in Chapter 4. References to the majority of sources upon which I have relied in preparing this report will be found in Chapter 4 in the brief synopses that precede the descriptions of the specimens of mescalbeans attributed to each of the groups known to have employed these seeds.

To date, mescalbeans have been recovered from the cultural deposits of sixteen prehistorically inhabited caves and rockshelters in southwestern Texas, southeastern New Mexico, and central Coahuila, Mexico. All these sites are located within the area where Sophora secundiflora occurs naturally (see Fig. 4). The cultural deposits from which mescalbeans have been recovered range in date from around 7000 B.C. to the historic period, indicating a long association between the prehistoric

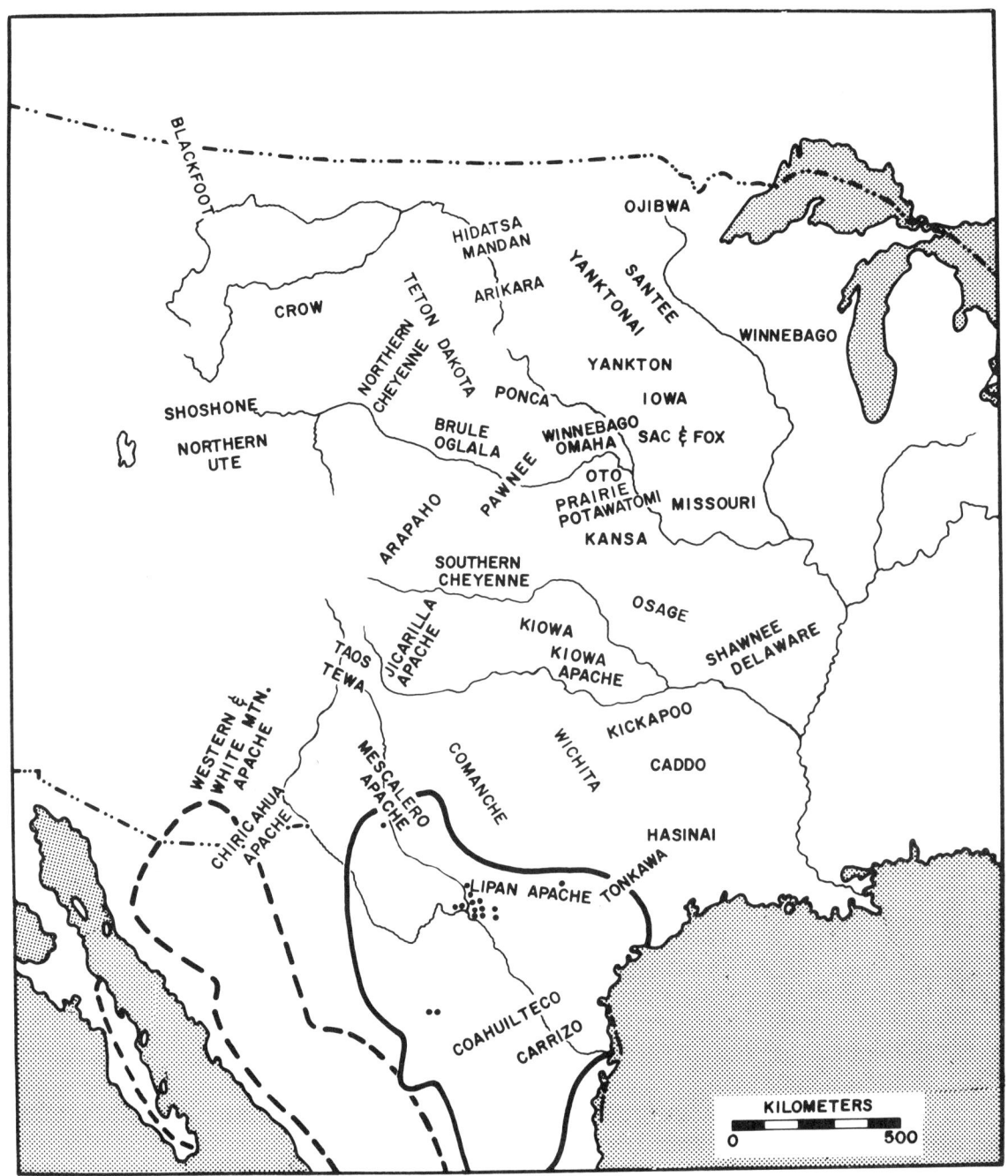

Figure 4. Approximate locations of Indian groups discussed in text. The solid heavy line indicates the limits of the distribution of Sophora secundiflora, the broken heavy line, that of Erythrina flabelliformis. The dots that appear within the solid heavy line mark the location of archaeological sites from which mescalbeans have been recovered.

inhabitants of this region and the Sophora secundiflora plant (Jones and Merrill n.d.). Unfortunately, the available archaeological evidence provides few insights into how these prehistoric peoples used mescalbeans. Only two sites--both located in Val Verde County, southwestern Texas--have yielded specimens of mescalbeans that exhibit evidence of having been treated preferentially. These specimens--a loincloth with mescalbeans attached to its fringe and a twined bag containing thirty-eight mescalbeans along with a variety of utilitarian and apparently non-utilitarian items--are pictured and described in Chapter 4 (specimens 1 and 2).

The loincloth provides unimpeachable evidence that the Archaic inhabitants of southwestern Texas attached mescalbeans to articles of clothing. The intended use of the twined bag and its contents is subject to more diverse interpretations. Some have proposed that the bag constitutes a medicine bundle and have interpreted the inclusion of mescalbeans in it as suggesting that the prehistoric inhabitants of the area ascribed to mescalbeans some degree of symbolic importance and perhaps employed them in ritualized contexts (Butler 1948:19-20; Campbell 1958: 157; Adovasio and Fry 1976:95). The presence of utilitarian items like flaking tools and fiber cordage suggests alternatively that the bag was a tool kit and that the mescalbeans, because of their toxic properties, may have been employed as a poison in some subsistence-related activity. The bag, of course, could have been both tool kit and medicine bundle, but this equivocation sheds no light on why the mescalbeans were included in the bag in the first place.

The remainder of mescalbeans recovered from archaeological sites have been found without any direct association with cultural materials that would reveal the reasons for their presence. Since Sophora secundiflora plants currently are found in close proximity to many of these sites and presumably were similarly located in times past, natural agents such as rain, flood waters, wind, and pack rats cannot be discounted as potentially responsible for introducing mescalbeans into these sites, particularly those yielding only a few mescalbeans (Jones and Merrill n.d.). Nonetheless, it is likely that some of the mescalbeans found in these caves and rockshelters were introduced intentionally by the human occupants of these sites, though their purposes for doing so remain unclear. Most writers have assumed that the mere presence of mescalbeans in these prehistoric habitation sites indicates that the human inhabitants consumed mescalbeans as a psychotropic substance. But this assumption is based on an ethnographic analogy with Indian groups who are known to have consumed mescalbeans for such purposes during the historic period, and there is no direct archaeological evidence to support it. On the other hand, it is obvious that the kind of evidence required to document conclusively that the prehistoric inhabitants of this area ingested mescalbeans would be hard to come by archaeologically. Archaeological sites within this same area have yielded specimens of both Lophophora williamsii and Ariocarpus fissuratus, neither of which are known to have been employed widely or very significantly for any purposes other than as psychotropic agents. The presence of these two kinds of "peyote" cacti suggests rather strongly that the prehistoric inhabitants of this area employed psychotropic plants and may have utilized mescalbeans for similar purposes (Jones and Merrill n.d.). In addition, it is reasonable to assume that the inhabitants of the area where Sophora secundiflora naturally occurs would have discovered and possibly exploited the psychotropic properties of mescalbeans long before Indian groups living outside this area. Circumstantially, then, the consumption of mescalbeans for their psychotropic properties by at least some of the prehistoric Indian groups living within the area where mescalbeans naturally occur seems likely.

The loincloth with mescalbeans attached to its fringe constitutes an important prehistoric precedent for the use of mescalbeans as seed beads. During the historic period, Indian groups inhabiting portions of northern Mexico, the American Southwest, the Great Basin-Plateau area, the northern, central, and southern Plains, Texas, and the Prairie region of what is now the United States all used mescalbeans as seed beads (see Fig. 3 and Table 1). In fact, all historic Indian groups who have been familiar with mescalbeans and for whom an adequate record of their material culture exists have employed mescalbeans in this fashion.

As groups previously unfamiliar with mescalbeans have come in contact with groups who employ mescalbeans, they too have begun using them. Such was the case with the several Algonquian-speaking groups displaced from the eastern United States into the Trans-Mississippi West. Similarly, mounted Basin-Plateau groups like the Shoshone probably began wearing mescalbeans only after they ventured out onto the Plains in search of buffalo and adopted more or less typical Plains Indian attire.

In addition, both the concentration of Indian groups from widely dispersed regions of the country in Oklahoma and the development of more efficient communication and transportation systems have led to the rather recent diffusion of mescalbeans to a number of groups who presumably had no previous acquaintance with these seeds. This recent diffusion of mescalbeans has been stimulated in particular by the fact that they have become important items of ritual paraphernalia in such modern pantribal movements as the Peyote Religion and the Gourd Dance (La Barre 1969; Howard 1976: 249-50). Today, mescalbeans, especially in the form of bandoleers, are standard elements of contemporary Indian dress and seem assured a prominent place in the future material culture of North American Indian groups.

While the most widespread and continuous purpose for which North American Indian groups have employed mescalbeans is as seed beads, a substantial number of groups have utilized mescalbeans in other ways as well. The Cheyenne, Comanche, and Kickapoo are known to employ mescalbeans for therapeutic purposes--the Cheyenne as an "eye-wash," the Comanche and Kickapoo to cure earaches. Other groups may have used mescalbeans similarly though the ethnographic record is silent in this regard. However, with the possible exceptions of the Comanche and certain Apachean groups, no Plain, Basin-Plateau, or Southwestern Indian groups are reported ever to have consumed mescalbeans on a regular or formal basis. Some of the Comanche bands may have included mescalbeans in an emetic and purgative decoction consumed during the celebration of their first fruits ceremonies, and the Mescalero and Chiricahua Apaches reportedly mixed mescalbeans on occasion with their corn beer. Otherwise, the consumption of mescalbeans or decoctions prepared from them was restricted to Indian groups who inhabited Texas and the Prairies of the United States. The Coahuilteco, Hasinai Caddo, and Tonkawa--all inhabiting portions of southern and eastern Texas during the early historic period--apparently ate mescalbeans in communal ceremonies in which both men and women participated. The Coahuilteco and Hasinai Caddo possibly consumed mescalbeans in conjunction with peyote during performance of these ceremonies; the Tonkawa maintained a separate peyote ceremony called the "wild hog dance" (Gotschet 1884:82).

By far the most elaborate symbolism and ceremonialism surrounding the use of mescalbeans in native North America was developed and maintained by those Caddoan- and Siouan-speaking groups who inhabited the southern and central Prairies of the United States. Among these groups, the use of mescalbeans apparently was restricted almost entirely to members of what has been termed the mescalbean medicine society, and the consumption of mescalbeans is believed to have taken place for the most part only in the context of this society's ceremonies. The Wichita seem to have been responsible for developing and originally diffusing this medicine society to the more northerly Prairie groups and to have served as prominent middlemen in the trade of mescalbeans to these groups (Jones and Merrill n.d.).

As would be expected in the case of any ceremonial complex widely diffused across linguistic and cultural boundaries, the various mescalbean medicine societies and the beliefs and practices they maintained varied from group to group. But with the possible exception of the Omaha, all Prairie groups from whom a description of their mescalbean medicine society exists consumed mescalbeans or a mescalbean decoction during at least some of the performances of their mescalbean medicine society ceremonies. Among the Siouan-speaking Ponca, Iowa, and Oto, all members of the mescalbean medicine society apparently drank a decoction of mescalbeans each time the society performed its ceremonies. The Iowa and Oto seem to have experienced only emesis, purging, and perhaps stimulation as a result while the Ponca are reported to have received visions on occasion. The Caddoan-speaking Pawnee and Wichita similarly associated the consumption of mescalbeans with the receipt of visions, but they appear to have allowed only their novitiates to consume mescalbeans for such purposes and these individuals only at the time of their initiation into the society. The Prairie Potawatomi, an Algonquian-speaking group who moved west of the Mississippi around 1835, also consumed a decoction of mescalbeans in the context of their "Throwing-Out-Medicine Ceremony." This ceremony and the accompanying use of mescalbeans probably was adopted from one of the Prairie groups, possibly the Pawnee, after the Prairie Potawatomi's arrival in Nebraska. Other displaced Algonquian-speaking groups like the Sac, Fox, Shawnee, and Delaware are not reported to have ever consumed mescalbeans although they did employ them as seed beads, as "power" objects carried as fetishes, or as elements included in their medicine bundles.

Underlying the historic North American Indians' diversity of uses for mescalbeans were several general beliefs and symbolic associations that were maintained by the majority of the Indian groups who were familiar with mescalbeans. Most if not all these groups believed that mescalbeans were living, sentient beings, capable of reproducing and initiating action on their own (Jones and Merrill n.d.). Groups such as the Omaha, Iowa, Oto, and Ponca gave material expression to this belief by carefully perforating the leather packets they manufactured to hold mescalbeans, so that the mescalbeans inside could breathe and see out.

Also widespread was the association between mescalbeans and deer ceremonialism, particularly among the Prairie groups who maintained mescalbean medicine societies. Wichita and Pawnee referred to their mescalbean ceremonies as Deer (or Elk) Dances (as did the Tonkawa, a non-Prairie group), and most of the other recorded Prairie mescalbean medicine society ceremonies were replete with deer symbolism.

Perhaps more widely distributed than this deer-mescalbean ceremonialism was the association of mescalbeans with horses. Several groups administered either whole mescalbeans or mescalbean decoctions to their horses to cure them or to enhance their swiftness. In addition, many groups referred to mescalbeans as horses and believed that mescalbeans could guarantee success in horse raiding expeditions. Since many of the raiding expeditions engaged in by Plains and Prairie groups during the historic period were motivated primarily by the desire to capture horses, mescalbeans also came to be associated with raiding activities (Jones and Merrill n.d.).

The association between mescalbeans and raiding derived from several sources in addition to the above chain of associations. Mescalbeans usually are red in color, and many Plains and Prairie groups associated the color red with warfare in their scheme of color classification. Additionally, the fact that mescalbeans are extremely durable seeds led several groups to effect an analogical transfer of this quality of hardness to their bullets, their projectile points, and their bodies (Dorsey 1884:349; Howard 1965:123). They felt that if this tranfer could be accomplished, their bullets, arrows, and lances would easily penetrate the bodies of their enemies while their own bodies would be impenetrable. Thus, mescalbeans were believed to enhance the possibility of achieving success in hostile encounters.

The preceding overview of the uses of mescalbeans in aboriginal North America indicates that North American Indian groups have employed those seeds since prehistoric times and that their use of them during this vast period has been characterized by both continuity and innovation. The longstanding popularity of mescalbeans can be attributed primarily to the fact that they are suitable for use both as a psychotropic substance and as seed beads. The prehistoric groups who inhabited the area where the Sophora secundiflora plant naturally occurs probably employed mescalbeans for both purposes. But the widespread diffusion of mescalbeans among North American Indian groups that seems to have begun sometime during the late proto-historic or early historic periods probably derived its impetus more from the physical attractiveness of mescalbeans than from their chemical constituents (Jones and Merrill n.d.). The important role of mescalbeans as items of North American Indian material culture is indicated in the following chapter.

II. MESCALBEANS IN NORTH AMERICAN INDIAN MATERIAL CULTURE

In Tables 1, 2, and 3 I have summarized the evidence that I have at present regarding the North American Indians' employment of mescalbeans as items of material culture. These tables are based on information from five sources: (1) my notes on the museum specimens of mescalbeans that I have personally examined; (2) descriptions of specimens examined by Volney H. Jones; (3) unpublished notes on mescalbean specimens examined by other individuals; (4) photographs depicting various North American Indian individuals wearing mescalbeans; and (5) published descriptions of the North American Indians' use of mescalbeans. This information, together with the sources from which it is derived, is presented in detail in Chapter 4.

I have arranged the groups in Tables 1, 2, and 3 roughly according to their geographical location and culture area affiliation: southern Texas groups appear first, followed by groups from the Prairies and the eastern margins of the Plains, then the High Plains groups, and finally groups that inhabited portions of the Basin-Plateau and the North American Southwest. This particular arrangement was chosen because a group's manner of using mescalbeans tended to vary somewhat according to location and cultural affiliation. Before commenting upon the contents of these tables and their implications for understanding the use of mescalbeans in native North America, it is necessary to point out some of the major problems concerning the data upon which these tables are based.

SOME QUALIFICATIONS

The collections of American museums do not equally represent all the American Indian groups who employed mescalbeans nor does the published material describe the use of mescalbeans in material culture in comparable detail for all groups. Further, it is certain that not all material culture items associated with mescalbeans by any given group are represented in museum collections or described in the published record. As a result, it is impossible to determine with any degree of certainty the entire range of uses for which a given group employed mescalbeans. Table 1, then, indicates the minimum rather than the total number of categories of items that the represented groups associated with mescalbeans.

For several groups, the only record of their familiarity with or employment of mescalbeans for a certain purpose is preserved in photographs. Unfortunately, many of these photographs were taken in studios (often in Washington, D.C.) with the photographers sometimes providing the clothing donned by their subjects. Since these costumes frequently consisted of several items of distinct cultural origins, their authenticity and the use of mescalbeans among the groups represented by individuals so pictured is subject to question.

In addition, in most cases I have been unable to determine the identity of all the seeds that appear in these photographs. Unless otherwise noted, I have employed photographs as evidence of the use of mescalbeans only in those cases where the distinctive seed scars of mescalbeans are clearly visible. However, usually the seed scars of only a few of the seeds present in a photograph are visible. Even though these seeds may resemble in all other particulars the seeds positively identifiable as mescalbeans, it is only on the basis of their seed scars that mescalbeans can be definitely distinguished from the seeds of Erythrina flabelliformis (see Fig. 1). As a result, it is impossible in most cases to state unequivocally that all the seeds portrayed in a given photograph are mescalbeans.

Similarly, the catalogue and accession information associated with museum specimens of mescalbeans usually are less detailed than is desirable. Sometimes specimens are identified only by a very general ethnic label such as "Sioux," rendering impossible attempts to assign them to more localized and, for the purposes of this study, more relevant ethnic groupings. In addition, the catalogue information frequently fails to reveal when or where a given item was manufactured or even when or where it was collected. The failure of most specimens to be associated with a date of manufacture is particularly unfortunate, since, as a result, it is exceedingly difficult to gauge the degree to which the use of mescalbeans varied through time. Because most museum specimens of mescalbeans were collected during the reservation period, it is uncertain whether some groups employed mescalbeans in their traditional homelands or only after being placed on reservations.

The accompanying catalogue information also frequently fails to reveal what categories of individuals--children, adults, males, females, or special individuals within these categories--employed these items and in what contexts they did so. As a result, the information presented in

Table 3 often is based more on my interpretations of the data than on explicit statements regarding the age and sex of the individuals who employed mescalbeans within each of the groups represented. Table 3 also fails to reflect the more subtle variations in use that may have occurred within a given group. For instance, in this table I have not indicated modern as opposed to more traditional usage. This is particularly misleading in the case of groups like the Pawnee, among whom women apparently did not employ mescalbeans prior to the twentieth century but have done so subsequently. Similarly, the categories of individuals who had access to mescalbeans as indicated in Table 3 often varied with context, with men (and perhaps specially designated women) employing mescalbeans in esoteric contexts while the populace in general used mescalbeans in less esoteric settings. The usefulness as well as the faults of Table 3 derive from its intent to reflect the use of mescalbeans in all contexts--as items of material culture and otherwise. I have attempted to compensate for the resultant inflexibility of this table in the accompanying text.

MESCALBEANS AND MATERIAL CULTURE

Concepts of beauty can be among the most provincial of values: what the members of one culture consider to be the epitome of beauty frequently is perceived by the members of another as bizarre, tasteless, or even ugly. Yet mescalbeans have caught the aesthetic fancy of members of a multitude of cultures, both North American Indian and European in origin. I believe that the widespread appeal of mescalbeans resides to a large degree in an appreciation of their formal and natural simplicity. Their basic ovoid shape and their solid red to maroon color are unbroken by elaborate embellishments. Being natural objects, mescalbeans are non-cultural and therefore appropriate for use in a theoretically infinite number of cultural settings. Their simple beauty, coupled with their extreme durability, renders them particularly suitable for seed beads, the manner in which they have been employed most widely and persistently in native North America.

The theories of beauty and concepts of decorative space maintained by the North American Indian groups who employed mescalbeans are not readily available. Nonetheless, the mescalbean specimens upon which the present study is based suggest that there was general agreement among most of the represented American Indian groups regarding what spaces were appropriate for the attachment of mescalbeans and how the mescalbeans so employed should look.

The cross-cultural redundancy in North American Indian use of mescalbeans can be attributed largely to the fact that the general styles of clothing and other material culture items did not vary considerably among these groups. By far the most popular use of mescalbeans among North American Indian groups has been as seed beads strung into bandoleers and necklaces (see Figs. 1, 11, 15, 16, 17, 20). The majority of Indian groups known to have been familiar with mescalbeans employed them in this fashion. In addition, it is most notably as bandoleers and necklaces that mescalbeans have been incorporated into the paraphernalia of the Peyote Religion and Gourd Dance and diffused along with these paraphernalia to groups previously unfamiliar with mescalbeans.

The other purposes for which American Indian groups employed mescalbeans tended to be distributed in more circumscribed areas. Particularly prominent and enjoying a fairly wide distribution was the practice of attaching mescalbeans to items of apparel (most frequently shirts, leggings, and dresses) or other articles like pouches and hair ornaments. The use of mescalbeans as attachments to such items of material culture was most widely distributed among those Indian groups who inhabited the Plains, Southwest, and perhaps portions of the Basin-Plateau areas of North America. The principal means by which mescalbeans were attached to clothing and accessories was by a leather string passing through a perforation in the seed, with the string in turn being attached to the article, usually as fringe. In fact, the presence of fringe on an item of material culture serves as a most reliable marker of the spaces on that item that were judged appropriate for decorative elaboration in general and the attachment of mescalbeans in particular. Of course, fringe designates decorative space primarily because it was itself a decorative elaboration, though in some cases it served practical ends as well. For example, the long leather strings looped through many of the leggings examined during the period of investigation served to taper the leggings as well as to provide loose ends by means of which mescalbeans and other items could be attached to them.

Mescalbeans were not the only items that Indian groups in the Plains and adjacent regions attached to the fringe of their clothing and other accouterments, nor did their use of mescalbeans in this fashion represent a stylistic innovation. These groups employed a wide variety of objects as attachments, including such "traditional" things as shells, elk teeth, feathers, bear claws, and bits of fur, together with European-introduced items like glass and metal trade beads and small metal springs. If, as seems likely, the majority of Indian groups living in these areas first gained access to mescalbeans in the late proto-historic or early historic periods (Jones and Merrill n.d.), the practice of attaching items to the fringe of objects of material culture would have long preceded the introduction of mescalbeans. As a result, mescalbeans, after becoming available, would simply have been incorporated as seed beads into the class of items already used for such purposes.

While several of the Prairie groups are reported to have employed mescalbean seed beads as attachments to their clothing and other articles, the use of mescalbeans in this fashion seems to have been much more limited among these groups than among the Indian groups of the Plains. In fact, the majority of Prairie groups who were familiar with mescalbeans tended to employ them rather esoterically and seem to have ascribed more symbolic significance to mescalbeans than did Indian groups in other areas. The nature of this cross-cultural variation in the use of mescalbeans will be discussed in more detail in Chapter 3 below.

The general failure of groups living outside the Prairies to employ mescalbeans in a more esoteric fashion does not necessarily indicate that these groups ascribed no special significance to mescalbeans. Very little information is available regarding the beliefs about mescalbeans maintained by Indian groups in the Plains and adjacent regions. However, when such information exists, it almost always indicates that the groups in question considered mescalbeans to be "powerful" objects and attributed to them some degree of symbolic significance. For example, Comanche (Jones 1972:58) and Kiowa men are reported in modern times to have attached mescalbeans to their leggings, trousers, and moccasins to protect themselves from the contaminating effects of contact with menstrual blood.

It is impossible to determine if the mescalbeans attached to items of material culture were in all cases considered to provide similar protection for their wearers or were intended to express by their presence something of more general symbolic import. Nor, in most cases, is it possible to establish whether the use of mescalbeans on a particular item of material culture had significance only for the individual who made and used the article or if this significance was held in common by the members of the society as a whole. Undoubtedly the presence of mescalbeans and similar objects served to enhance the attractiveness of the items of material culture to which they were attached and can be considered to reflect at least the desire of the manufacturer to produce an aesthetically pleasing article. On the other hand, a number of the Indian groups under consideration also attached small medicine packets--composed of vegetal or mineral material wrapped in buckskin or cloth and presumably intended to provide protection for the wearer--to the fringe of many of the same articles to which they attached mescalbeans. The association of mescalbeans with these medicine packets suggests that they too were believed to have special significance and that the Indian groups who employed them in this fashion considered the fringed portions of their clothing and other articles the most appropriate spaces for attaching such objects. In view of the above considerations, it seems likely that both aesthetic and symbolic factors entered into the decision to attach mescalbeans to articles of material culture.

In addition to cross-cultural similarities in the North American Indians' employment of mescalbeans, there also seems to have been a general consensus among these groups regarding the criteria by which they selected mescalbeans for use on a particular item. The available evidence indicates that these groups generally preferred mescalbeans that were relatively large in size and deep maroon in color, though some individuals have expressed a preference for the lighter, yellowish-colored mescalbeans (Schultes 1937:141; Garland Blaine 1976:personal communication). However, a seemingly more important criterion in the selection of mescalbeans for attachment to any given article was that all the mescalbeans so employed display a general uniformity in size, shape, and color.

American Indians who employed mescalbeans apparently would not have regarded all mescalbeans as equally suitable for use as seed beads. Mescalbeans produced even by the same _Sophora secundiflora_ shrub tend to display a wide variety of sizes, shapes, and colors. I was able to document this variety by examining about two pounds of mescalbeans freshly gathered from _S. secundiflora_ shrubs near Del Rio, Texas, and kindly supplied by Mr. Emery C. Hahnert, Chief Naturalist of the Amistad Recreation Area. The mescalbeans in this lot varied in size from 0.8 to

1.5 cm in length and from 0.5 to 1.0 cm wide. The majority of the seeds displayed a light orangish-red color, though some bore darker red mottlings. Mescalbeans apparently darken as they age; seeds in the same lot definitely identifiable as being at least one year old were darker red in color than were freshly produced mescalbeans. However, none of the mescalbeans in this lot displayed the dark maroon color that is so characteristic of mescalbeans attached to museum specimens of North American Indian material culture.

It is likely that the color of mescalbeans varies from area to area within the natural range of <u>Sophora secundiflora</u>, with the mescalbeans that were traded to groups outside of this area being naturally darker in color than the ones collected from near Del Rio. I have been unable to investigate this possibility systematically. On the other hand, there is good reason to believe that this apparently most desirable deep maroon color was at least partially produced either through use or through intentional dry heating or boiling. My wife and I were able to darken the color of about twenty-five mescalbeans from a relatively light red to a deep maroon by covering them with cooking oil and baking them at 350°F in our oven for about fifteen minutes. Although the color of the treated mescalbeans closely approximated the color of most museum specimens of mescalbeans, they lacked the characteristic glossiness displayed by many of the latter seeds. It is possible that the mescalbeans employed as seed beads were polished before use, though the glossy finish could equally have been the result of the transference of body oils to the seeds during use.

Most of the mescalbeans examined had been perforated by means of a hot drill. My wife discovered that mescalbeans could be readily perforated with the heated end of a straightened paper clip and that this method of perforation was superior to any other method tried. However, heat perforation has its disadvantages. The use of a hot drill usually discolors the seed, particularly around the perforations, and sometimes cracks it, rendering it useless. Mescalbeans perforated in this fashion sometimes exude a sticky oil from their perforations, which spreads to the surface of the seed. Perhaps as a result of such undesirable "side effects" of the hot drill method of perforation, some individuals preferred to perforate their mescalbeans with a cold drill. The method of perforation selected seems to have been a matter of individual rather than cultural taste, though the use of a hot drill appears to have been the method most widely employed by North American Indian groups in general. Undoubtedly perforation of the very hard mescalbeans was facilitated by the availability of metal tools. Prior to the use of metal, the preferred method for perforating mescalbeans, at least among some groups, was to heat up the sharpened end of a piece of hard wood and apply it to the end of the mescalbean to be perforated. The piece of wood was successively heated and applied to the mescalbean until the seed was perforated (Garland Blaine 1976:personal communication). An alternative method for preparing mescalbean seed beads was to split rather than perforate them. The mescalbeans which appear on the prehistoric loincloth recovered in southwestern Texas (Specimen 1) were split longitudinally and slipped around the fringe of the loincloth. They remained attached to the fringe because they shrank as they dehydrated.

III. SOME ETHNOGRAPHIC PROBLEMS

The principal motivation for undertaking this research project was to secure information not available in the published literature that would provide insights into the distribution of mescalbean use among North American Indian groups and the manner in which these groups employed mescalbeans. Though museum collections often are ignored in ethnographic inquiries, the results of this project indicate that museum specimens can be invaluable sources of information in the solution of <u>certain kinds of problems</u> if the information so secured is employed judiciously. I emphasize <u>certain kinds of problems</u> because museum collections obviously do not contain the kinds of information needed to solve all the problems with which the ethnographer is confronted. For example, mescalbeans are more likely to be found in museum collections than are such things as kinship terminologies. But since non-material aspects of culture often find material expression, museum collections can provide insights into ethnographic problems of a non-material nature. Four major problems relating to the North American Indians' use of mescalbeans were addressed and at least partially solved during the course of this investigation. These problems, listed and then discussed in succession below, should provide an indication of the kinds of problems that can be approached with data from museum collections.

These four problems--or, more accurately, sets of problems--are as follows:

(1) How far beyond the natural range of Sophora secundiflora were mescalbeans traded among American Indian groups in the historic period? Along what routes did this trade take place? What groups were involved?

(2) What is the relationship between the North American Indians' use of mescalbeans and their employment of the very similar seeds of Erythrina flabelliformis?

(3) For what range of uses did North American Indian groups employ mescalbeans? How much did the use of mescalbeans vary cross-culturally among those North American Indian groups who were familiar with them? How can this cross-cultural variation be explained?

(4) What is the relationship between the North American Indians' use of mescalbeans and peyote and the ceremonialism they associated with these two plants in the pre-reservation and reservation periods?

THE DISTRIBUTION OF THE USE OF MESCALBEANS AMONG HISTORIC NORTH AMERICAN INDIAN GROUPS

The Sophora secundiflora plant reaches the northern limits of its natural distribution in southeastern New Mexico and central Texas (see Fig. 3). All the prehistoric habitation sites from which mescalbeans have been recovered are located south of these limits (see Fig. 4), suggesting that the use of mescalbeans in prehistoric times was restricted to groups located within or immediately adjacent to the area where mescalbeans naturally occur. In contrast, it is a well documented fact that, in historic times, mescalbeans were traded far beyond their area of natural distribution to groups inhabiting the region bounded by

Arizona and Utah on the west, Montana, North Dakato, and perhaps Canada on the north, and the states of Minnesota, Iowa, Missouri, Arkansas, and Louisiana on the east (see Fig. 4). A general idea of the boundaries of this area can be gleaned from published reports, but there are rather serious gaps in this literature. Specimens and photographs examined during the period of investigation fill in some of these gaps by documenting the use of mescalbeans in the material culture of several groups not reported previously to have employed mescalbeans.

Ironically, the groups who resided at the limits of the trade of mescalbeans also are, in most cases, among those groups for whom little or no information regarding their use of mescalbeans is available in the published record. For example, the Western Apache of eastern Arizona and the Shoshone located in the northeastern portions of the Great Basin are the westernmost groups known to have employed mescalbeans, but the use of mescalbeans by these groups is not documented at all in the published record. A similar situation exists for the Blackfoot and Dakota Sioux who resided at the northern limits of the areas within which mescalbeans were traded. The published record is more complete regarding the distribution of mescalbean use in the regions to the south and east. Published information, supplemented by unpublished data gathered during this investigation, indicates that most if not all historic Indian groups who inhabited the Plains, Prairies, and Texas areas of North America, at least one group located in the northeastern Great Basin, together with most of the Apachean groups and perhaps some of the Puebloan groups in the American Southwest were familiar with mescalbeans and employed them in one fashion or another (see Table 1).

Most of the published and unpublished information derives from the reservation period. As a result, it is impossible to determine just how far mescalbeans were traded in the pre-reservation period. Certainly Indian groups like the Delaware and Winnebago who were located during much of the historic period east of the Mississippi River are not suspected to have been familiar with mescalbeans prior to their extensive contact with Trans-Mississippian groups who employed mescalbeans. In addition, there is substantial evidence to indicate that the number of Indian groups that employed mescalbeans increased somewhat during the reservation period, particularly because mescalbeans became an important component of the paraphernalia of the Peyote Religion and, more recently, the Gourd Dance. In any case, the evidence suggests that mescalbeans were traded widely among Indian groups in the Prairies, Plains, and perhaps western and southern margins of the Plains prior to the inception of the reservation period.

It seems likely that most mescalbeans were traded primarily after they had been removed from their enclosing pods. However, the use of intact *Sophora secundiflora* pods has been documented among the Iowa, Oto, Oglala Sioux, Kiowa-Apache, and Western Apache, all of whom lived some distance beyond the natural range of *S. secundiflora*. All the pods except the Kiowa-Apache and Western Apache ones have been employed as ritually significant items, indicating that there may have been some demand for the mescalbean pods as well as for the mescalbeans themselves.

There appear to have been at least two major routes along which mescalbeans were traded during the pre-reservation period. The first, referred to here as the Prairie route, had its southern terminus among the Wichita, who lived immediately north of the area where mescalbeans naturally occur. For the more northerly located Prairie groups, the Wichita seem to have been the ultimate source of mescalbeans and much of the ritual and symbolism associated with them. The Oto for example, are reported to have procured their supply of mescalbeans "in some circuitous manner" from the Wichita (James 1905, vol. 16:217). Similarly, the available information suggests that the Pawnee, Iowa, and Omaha acquired mescalbean medicine societies and perhaps a portion of their supply of mescalbeans ultimately from the Wichita (Jones and Merrill n.d.). Of course, the Wichita themselves may have been the recipients of mescalbeans from groups located within the natural range of S. secundiflora or they may have secured their supply of mescalbeans during excursions into this area; since the ethnographic record is silent on this point, either or both alternatives are equally plausible.

The second route along which mescalbeans were traded--the Plains route--stretched north from the southern Plains and perhaps northern Mexico to the central and northern Plains. The Southern Plains groups, particularly the Comanche, probably were the ultimate source of mescalbeans for many of the Plains groups located to their north as well as the more Plains-oriented Great Basin groups. By the end of the eighteenth century, some of the southern Comanche bands were inhabiting areas of western Texas where mescalbeans naturally occur. In the nineteenth

TABLE 1. CATEGORIES OF ITEMS ASSOCIATED WITH MESCALBEANS BY GROUP

GROUP	DRESSES	HAIR ORNAMENTS	SHIRTS	LEGGINGS	POUCHES	NECKLACES AND BANDOLEERS	BRACELETS	PODS	PERFORATED PACKETS	MEDICINE BUNDLES - MESCALBEAN MEDICINE SOCIETY	MEDICINE BUNDLES - OTHER	OTHER CATEGORIES AND REMARKS
Prehistoric SW Texas											X(?)	Loincloth
Coahuilteco												No information
Tonkawa												No information
Caddo						X						
Wichita				X		X						
Pawnee					X	X	X(?)			X		
Iowa				X		X		X	X	X		
Oto						X		X	X	X		
Missouri						X(?)						
Kansa						X(?)						
Osage						X						
Omaha		X				X			X	X		
Ponca		X	X	X	X	X	X		X			Jackrabbit skin
Arikara						X						
Mandan						X						
Hidatsa						X						
Prairie Potawatomi	X		X	X		X	X					
Sac & Fox						X			X		X	
Shawnee						X						
Delaware												No information
Kickapoo			X			X						
Ojibwa						X						Cradle (?)
Winnebago						X						Peyote whistle
Sioux	X		X			X						Cradle, Headdress
Teton			X									
Brule	X	X	X									
Oglala						X		X				
Yankton	X					X						
Upper Yanktonai				X								

TABLE 1. CATEGORIES OF ITEMS ASSOCIATED WITH MESCALBEANS BY GROUP

GROUP	DRESSES	HAIR ORNAMENTS	SHIRTS	LEGGINGS	POUCHES	NECKLACES OR BANDOLEERS	BRACELETS	PODS	PERFORATED PACKETS	MEDICINE BUNDLES – MESCALBEAN MEDICINE SOCIETY	MEDICINE BUNDLES – OTHER	OTHER CATEGORIES AND REMARKS
Comanche	X					X						
Kiowa	X		X	X		X						Moccasins, Gourd rattle, Doll
Kiowa-Apache	X(?)		X	X	X	X						
Arapaho			X	X		X		X				
Cheyenne		X	X	X							X(?)	Loincloth(?), Hide painting Horse draping(?), Lance(?)
Northern Cheyenne	X					X						Doll
Southern Cheyenne		X(?)	X	X	X	X					X	
Crow	X(?)											Lance (?)
Blackfoot						X						
Shoshone			X									
Apache				X								
Lipan Apache												No information
Jicarilla Apache												No Informaion
Mescalero Apache						X						
Chiricahua Apache						X(?)						
Western Apache								X	X			
White Mountain Apache									X			
Santa Clara												No information
Taos						X						

century, the Comanche--as well as the Kiowa, Kiowa-Apache, and some of the Apache groups--were raiding deep into the natural range of S. secundiflora as far south as the Mexican states of Durango, Zacatecas, and San Luis Potosí (Stewart 1974:215-16; Smith 1961, 1962).

In addition to these north-south trade routes, there is some suggestion that mescalbeans were traded in an east to west direction from the southern Prairies and Plains to the American Southwest. Ford (1972) has documented the extensive trade that took place between nomadic Plains groups, particularly the Comanche, and the Tewa Pueblos of the Rio Grande Valley. He (1972: Table 2) lists mescalbeans among the goods supplied by the Comanche to the Tewa Pueblo of Santa Clara. The Osage also are believed to have supplied mescalbeans to Santa Clara (see Specimen 59 below). Similarly, Robbins, et al. (1916:69) report that the Comanche and "Pueblo Indians" engaged in the mutual trade of large red seeds, which supposedly grew on the Comanche, Kiowa, and Osage reservations in Oklahoma. The seed specimen associated with this information has been identified not as Sophora secundiflora but as Erythrina flabelliformis (Volney H. Jones 1973:personal communication). Neither of these plants grow in Oklahoma nor do they appear in the Pueblo region of New Mexico (see Fig. 2). The Comanche are known to have employed the seeds of E. flabelliformis (hereafter termed coralbeans) as seed beads, apparently on an interchangeable basis with mescalbeans (see Table 2), but there are a great many more mescalbeans than coralbeans associated with the museum specimens of Comanche provenience which were examined. Given the distribution of these two plants, the Comanche presumably would have had easier access to mescalbeans than to coralbeans. In fact, it is unclear where the Comanche secured their supply of coralbeans, although the Spanish and certain of the Apache groups are likely sources. Since mescalbeans and coralbeans so closely resemble one another and are therefore easily confused (see Fig. 1), Robbins, et al. or their informants might have concluded that the Comanche were dealing in only one kind of red seed when in reality possibly both mescalbeans and coralbeans were involved. In any case, it seems likely that the majority of red seeds brought by the Comanches to the New Mexico Pueblos were mescalbeans rather than coralbeans.

There is no evidence that an east-west trade route existed farther north, nor that any of the groups in the Prairie trade route engaged in the trade of mescalbeans with the groups in the Plains trade route. On the other hand, many of the groups who used mescalbeans considered them to be rather valuable trade items (Jones and Merrill n.d.). This fact, coupled with the fact that mescalbeans are readily transportable, suggests that the mescalbean-using groups could and would have freely engaged in trading them with one another when the opportunity arose.

MESCALBEANS AND CORALBEANS

The likelihood that both mescalbeans and coralbeans were being traded among groups in the American Southwest and Plains raises a second question: What was the relationship between the distribution of the use of mescalbeans and the distribution of the use of coralbeans in native North America? The available literature on the subject muddles more than clarifies this problem.

Although the Sophora secundiflora and Erythrina flabelliformis plants themselves bear little resemblance to one another, the ranges in size, shape, and color displayed by their respective seeds overlap. As a result, the only consistent distinguishing feature between mescalbeans and coralbeans is the form of their seed scars: the seed scar of the mescalbean is indented while that of the coralbean is exserted or flush with the remainder of the surface of the seed (see Fig. 2). Most reports discussing the use of what generally have been interpreted as mescalbeans are not accompanied by a competent botanical identification of the seeds in question, nor do they provide a description of these seeds that is sufficiently detailed to allow for an identification to be made now. Since many groups employed mescalbeans and coralbeans interchangeably, it is impossible in many cases to determine on the basis of the published information alone whether only one or both kinds of seeds were being employed.

The problem is complicated by the fact that several authors have reported that the Iowa, Oto, and Omaha employed the seeds of E. flabelliformis in association with the activities of what I have been referring to here as the mescalbean medicine society (Gilmore 1919:99, 140, 147; 1924:62; Skinner 1925:38; 1926:246). Since the Iowa are reported to have consumed these seeds, the identification of the seeds that many of the Prairie groups consumed in the context of their mescalbean medicine society ceremonies becomes problematical. Because the pharmacologic action of E. flabelliformis resembles in some particulars that of S.

secundiflora, the physiological effects reported to have followed the consumption of these seeds cannot be used to distinguish which of the two seeds was ingested (Jones and Merrill n.d.).

Fortunately, the museum specimens examined during this investigation appear to provide a suitable resolution of this problem (see Table 2). Specimens bearing coralbeans were found almost exclusively among groups who inhabited the Plains and Southwest--the Comanche, Arapaho, Cheyenne, and Chiricahua Apache (Specimens 4, 11, 25, 26, and 31)--while they were associated with the material culture of only two Prairie groups, the Wichita and the Osage. The Wichita specimen (Specimen 85) consists of a single coralbean strung along with eighty-eight mescalbeans into a "medicine string." The use of coralbeans by the Osage is documented in a photograph of an Osage man wearing a bandoleer that definitely includes coralbeans, metal trade beads, and perhaps mescalbeans as well (National Anthropological Archives, Smithsonian Institution, negative number 4066-B). The photograph was taken in 1905; no information exists regarding the Osage use of coralbeans prior to the twentieth century. The Oto and Omaha specimens that originally were identified as E. flabelliformis turned out on reexamination to be S. secundiflora; no coralbeans at all were discovered in association with specimens from the Iowa or any Prairie groups other than the Wichita and Osage. The only groups known to have consumed mescalbeans on a regular or formal basis inhabited the Prairies area or the region where Sophora secundiflora naturally occurs. Since coralbeans seem to have been exceedingly rare or perhaps totally absent

TABLE 2. THE ASSOCIATION ON <u>SOPHORA SECUNDIFLORA</u> AND <u>ERYTHRINA FLABELLIFORMIS</u> ON PARTICULAR ITEMS OF MATERIAL CULTURE BY GROUP

Group	Sophora secundiflora alone	Erythrina flabelliformis alone	S. secundiflora and E. flabelliformis
Prehistoric SW Texas	X		
Coahuilteco	X(?)		
Tonkawa	X		
Caddo	X		
Wichita	X		X
Pawnee	X		
Iowa	X		
Oto	X		
Missouri	X(?)		
Kansa	X(?)		
Osage	X		X
Omaha	X		
Ponca	X		
Arikara	X		
Mandan	X		
Hidatsa	X		
Prairie Potawatomi	X		
Sac & Fox	X		
Shawnee	X		
Delaware	X		
Kickapoo	X		
Ojibwa	X		
Winnebago	X		

TABLE 2. THE ASSOCIATION OF <u>SOPHORA SECUNDIFLORA</u> AND <u>ERYTHRINA FLABELLIFORMIS</u> ON PARTICULAR ITEMS OF MATERIAL CULTURE BY GROUP

Group	<u>Sophora secundiflora</u> alone	<u>Erythrina flabelliformis</u> alone	<u>S. secundiflora</u> and <u>E. flabelliformis</u>
Sioux	X		
Teton	X		
Brule	X		
Oglala	X		
Yankton	X		
Upper Yanktonai	X		
Comanche	X		X
Kiowa	X		
Kiowa-Apache	X		
Arapaho	X		X
Cheyenne	X		
Northern Cheyenne	X	X	X
Southern Cheyenne	X		X(?)
Crow	X(?)		
Blackfoot	X(?)		
Shoshone	X		
Apache	X		
Lipan Apache	X(?)		
Jicarilla Apache	X(?)		
Mescalero Apache	X		
Chiricahua Apache	X	X	

TABLE 2. THE ASSOCIATION ON SOPHORA SECUNDIFLORA AND ERYTHRINA FLABELLIFORMIS ON PARTICULAR ITEMS OF MATERIAL CULTURE BY GROUP

Group	Sophora secundiflora alone	Erythrina flabelliformis alone	S. secundiflora and E. flabelliformis
Western Apache	X(?)		
White Mountain Apache	X(?)		
Santa Clara	X		
Taos	X(?)		

among the majority of these groups, it can be said with some certainty that the seeds consumed by these groups were mescalbeans rather than coralbeans.

However, before the matter is closed, it should be noted that the seeds of a third legume, Abrus precatorius L., were discovered in association with Prairie mescalbean medicine society paraphernalia. These small red and black seeds were included in mescalbean medicine society bundles collected from the Iowa (Specimen 40) and Omaha (Specimen 58). Abrus precatorius seeds are employed in many parts of the world in the manufacture of necklaces and the treatment of certain physical ailments (Lampe and Fagerström 1968:60-62; Standley 1928:212), but I have yet to encounter a published reference to the use of these seeds by any North American Indian groups. Due to their red color, these seeds could have been incorporated by the Prairie groups into the category "red medicine", the term applied to mescalbeans by most of these groups. Thus, in those cases where a more detailed description or identification of the seeds in question is lacking, there is little way of determining whether the Prairie groups were employing mescalbeans, the seeds of A. precatorius, or both kinds of seeds. Personally, I feel that the seeds of A. precatorius, in contrast to mescalbeans, were relatively rare among the Prairie groups and, when they were available, probably were employed only as items of material culture rather than as ingredients in emetic, purgative, or otherwise psychotropic decoctions. This conclusion is based on both geographical and pharmacological considerations.

While A. precatorius enjoys almost worldwide distribution, it is confined for the most part to more tropical and subtropical regions. It grows no closer to the Prairies than the Caribbean islands and the Mexican state of Veracruz. As a result, the Prairie groups probably would not have had ready access to a supply of these seeds. This circumstance is reflected in the fact that A. precatorius seeds were associated with only two of the numerous museum specimens of Prairie provenience examined during the investigation. No information exists which would reveal how the Iowa and Omaha acquired these seeds. Given their popularity as necklace beads they probably were imported into the continental United States through established commercial channels and ultimately traded to the Iowa and Omaha.

Regardless of how these groups secured Abrus precatorius seeds, it is unlikely that they consumed them. These seeds contain, in addition to at least two alkaloids, the highly toxic protein abrin, a lethal dose of which has been estimated at 0.01 mg/kg (Ghosal and Dutta 1971; Lampe and Fagerström 1968:60-62). Of course, the extreme toxicity of these seeds does not preclude the possibility that the Prairie groups were consuming them in minute quantities, but this level of toxicity would render the determination of a suitable but non-fatal dosage difficult and the effects of consumption unpredictable. In view of these considerations, it seems likely that the 'red medicine' consumed by the Prairie groups in the context of their mescalbean medicine society ceremonies were the seeds of Sophora secundiflora rather than those of Abrus precatorius or Erythrina flabelliformis.

CROSS-CULTURAL VARIATION IN THE USE OF MESCALBEANS

The information presented in Table 1 indicates that were was considerable cross-cultural variation in the range of uses to which North American Indian groups put mescalbeans. Yet this variation seems to exhibit a pattern, for upon closer examination, two groupings emerge from the data. These groupings possibly express certain general tendencies among the Indian groups represented to use mescalbeans for certain categories of items but not for others. I have labelled the two groupings as esoteric and exoteric according to the degree to which the items associated with mescalbeans appeared in restricted contexts or were used by specified categories of individuals rather than by the population at large. The esoteric uses of mescalbeans are associated with those Indian groups who inhabited the Prairie regions of the United States while the exoteric uses are associated with groups living outside the Prairies in the Plains, Southwest, and Basin-Plateau.

The Prairie groups seem to have restricted their use of mescalbeans largely to those categories of items that were endowed with large amounts of ritual significance. These groups characteristically employed mescalbeans as components in their medicine bundles or as seed beads strung together to form necklaces and bandoleers. Though some Prairie groups also attached mescalbeans to items of clothing, they generally appear to have done this rather infrequently. In contrast, the use of mescalbeans as attachments to clothing and other less esoteric articles was characteristic of groups living outside the Prairies. Like the Prairie groups, the non-Prairie groups employed mescalbeans frequently in the manufacture of necklaces and bandoleers, but unlike the Prairie groups, most of the non-Prairie groups associated mescalbeans with items that were intended for use by females and children--e.g., dresses, cradles, dolls, and children's necklaces. The evidence on hand indicates that few if any of the Prairie groups extended the use of mescalbeans to women and children in general, at least during the pre-reservation period (see Table 3). Moreover, of all the non-Prairie groups only the Northern Cheyenne and possibly the Arapaho are known to have included mescalbeans in their medicine bundles.

The degree to which a group employed mescalbeans esoterically in their material culture may reflect rather faithfully in material terms the degree to which the group imposed restrictions on the use of mescalbeans in general. Most of the Prairie groups appear to have restricted access to mescalbeans almost exclusively to men and, more specifically to the members (usually men but some women also) of their mescalbean medicine societies. Mrs. Effie Blaine (in Weltfish 1937:107) states explicitly that among the Pawnee only the members of the Pawnee Deer Society (the local variant of the mescalbean medicine society) had access to and were allowed to use mescalbeans. Though comparable statements are lacking for the other Prairie groups who maintained mescalbean medicine societies, the failure to discover evidence--either published or unpublished--that would indicate a more general use of mescalbeans among most of these groups suggests that they too imposed similar restrictions.

TABLE 3. AGE AND SEX OF MESCALBEAN USERS BY GROUP

Group	Age of Users		Sex of Users	
	Child	Adult	Female	Male
Prehistoric SW Texas		X		X
Coahuilteco		X(?)	X	X(?)
Tonkawa		X	X	X
Caddo		X	X	X
Wichita		X		X
Pawnee		X	X	X
Iowa		X		X
Oto		X	X(?)	X
Missouri		X(?)		X(?)
Kansa		X		X
Osage		X		X
Omaha	X	X	X	X
Ponca		X		X
Arikara		X		X
Mandan		X		X
Hidatsa		X		X
Prairie Potawatomi		X	X	X
Sac & Fox		X		X
Shawnee		X		X
Delaware	−	−	−	−
Kickapoo	X(?)	X	X(?)	X
Ojibwa	X(?)	X	X(?)	X
Winnebago		X		X
Sioux	X	X	X	X
Teton		X		X
Brule		X	X	X
Oglala		X		X
Yankton		X	X	X

− = no information

TABLE 3. AGE AND SEX OF MESCALBEAN USERS BY GROUP

Group	Age of Users		Sex of Users	
	Child	Adult	Female	Male
Upper Yanktonai		X		X
Comanche	X	X	X	X
Kiowa	X	X	X	X
Kiowa-Apache		X	X(?)	X
Arapaho		X		X
Cheyenne	X	X	X	X
Northern Cheyenne		X	X	X
Southern Cheyenne	X(?)	X	X(?)	X
Crow		X(?)	X(?)	X(?)
Blackfoot		X		X
Shoshone		X		X
Apache		X	X(?)	X
Lipan Apache	−	−	−	−
Jicarilla Apache	−	−	−	−
Mescalero Apache		X	X(?)	X
Chiricahua Apache		X	X(?)	X(?)
Western Apache		X	X(?)	X(?)
White Mountain Apache		X	X(?)	X(?)
Santa Clara	−	−	−	−
Taos	X	X(?)		X

− = no information

The existence of the restrictions on the use of mescalbeans that apparently were imposed by the Prairie groups perhaps can be explained by considering the nature of the institution of Prairie medicine societies together with the kinds of meanings which these Prairie groups may have assigned to mescalbeans. Among the Prairie groups, membership in medicine societies was restricted since not all individuals within the larger society were equally qualified for admission. An individual usually gained entry into a medicine society either through purchase or inheritance or both. However, access to positions in these societies was to a great degree controlled by the kin-based groups who composed the larger society. The right to purchase a position in one of these medicine societies frequently was the prerogative of certain kin-based groups and an individual usually had to rely on his kinsmen for the goods which comprised his admission fee (Jones and Merrill n.d.).

By controlling access to positions in the medicine societies, the kin-based groups also controlled access to certain avenues of gaining wealth. The medicine societies were curing societies and their members often received rather extravagant payments in return for performing their cures. On a less materialistic level, the medicine societies also possessed medicine bundles, the contents of which were believed to enhance an individual's chances of achieving success in his daily affairs. Most if not all the Prairie groups believed that simply possessing mescalbeans would guarantee such things as good health and success in capturing horses or that consuming them would establish contact with spiritual beings who could endow the individual with the knowledge required to enhance his abilities in his everyday life. Mescalbeans were central components in the paraphernalia of the various Prairie mescalbean medicine societies and most of the Prairie groups probably received their first substantial supplies of mescalbeans in the context of this society. As a result, it is likely that the members of the mescalbean medicine societies would have been among the first individuals in their group to possess mescalbeans and subsequently would have attempted to retain their control over access to mescalbeans. Their success in this regard seems to be indicated by the limited range of uses for which the Prairie groups employed mescalbeans in their material culture.

Even some of those Prairie groups who did not maintain a mescalbean medicine society, like the Sac and Fox, appear to have placed restrictions, if not on the individuals who could use mescalbeans, at least on the contexts within which mescalbeans could be employed. The restricted use of mescalbeans among such groups may have derived from their presumed adaption of mescalbeans and the accompanying ideology from Prairie groups who maintained mescalbean medicine societies.

The more general, or exoteric, use of mescalbeans found among the non-Prairie groups no doubt partially reflects the fact that none of these groups maintained a mescalbean medicine society. As a result, they could not have employed mescalbeans as esoteric items of mescalbean medicine society paraphernalia nor would there have been individuals among them who maintained a vested interest in limiting access to mescalbeans as perhaps did the members of the Prairie mescalbean medicine societies.

Since none of the groups in the Plains, Southwest, or Basin-Plateau areas seem to have consumed mescalbeans in connection with their quest for visionary experiences, they would not have developed the elaborate symbolism that would be expected to arise out of such use of mescalbeans. There is no explicit statement indicating that any of the non-Prairie groups restricted the use of mescalbeans to any particular contexts or any categories of individuals. Instead, these groups appear to have believed that mescalbeans were beneficial to all individuals who possessed them and that all members of the groups should have access to mescalbeans.

The mescalbean medicine societies, together with the majority of Prairie medicine societies, declined in importance and eventually disappeared following the placement of the Prairie groups onto reservations. It might be presumed that the demise of the mescalbean medicine societies was accompanied by the disappearance, or at least a relaxing, of the restrictions these groups imposed on the use of mescalbeans. It might also be expected that the Prairie groups adopted some of the more exoteric uses of mescalbeans from the non-Prairie groups with whom they established close and constant contact on their reservations. Yet the available evidence fails to indicate that the categories of individuals who had access to mescalbeans radically changed between the pre-reservation and reservation periods.

Both Pawnee and Oto women are reported to have worn mescalbean necklaces in the twentieth century (Garland and Martha Blaine 1976:personal communication). In addition, a girl's hair ornament collected among the

Omaha in 1930 (Specimen 57) substantiates the use of mescalbeans during the reservation period by another category of individuals--girls--who may not have been allowed to employ mescalbeans previously. However, there is some indication that Omaha and Oto women may have used mescalbeans as fetishes before the inception of the reservation period (Dorsey 1894: 416), and it is certain that the Omaha mescalbean medicine society included women among its members (Dorsey 1884:350). It is also possible that certain Prairie groups--the Wichita, Iowa, Ponca, and Prairie Potawatomi--may have adopted the practice of attaching mescalbeans to articles of clothing from the Southern Plains groups with whom they came in contact. Some of the articles of Prairie clothing discussed in Chapter 4 to which mescalbeans are attached are considered to be Southern Plains in style if not in origin. Unfortunately, it is practically impossible to gauge the degree to which the restrictions on the use of mescalbeans were rescinded among the Prairie groups in reservation times. The majority of the ethnographic specimens examined during this investigation and the bulk of the published information regarding mescalbean use by Prairie groups, while collected during the reservation period, are intended to illustrate the use of mescalbeans in pre-reservation rather than reservation times. I suspect that contemporary members of the Prairie groups considered here employ mescalbeans much more generally than did their ancestors during the pre-reservation period though I have little substantiating evidence.

MESCALBEANS AND PEYOTE

During the reservation period, mescalbeans have been integrated as items of material culture into the paraphernalia of the Peyote Religion and have been used widely in Peyote paraphernalia among Indian groups who have accepted the Peyote Religion. The prominence of mescalbeans in Peyote paraphernalia and the fact that the majority of the groups who adopted the Peyote Religion during the reservation period had been familiar with mescalbeans during the pre-reservation period has engendered considerable debate regarding the relationship between pre-reservation mescalbean medicine society ceremonialism and the peyote ceremonialism of the reservation period. Three principal positions have been advanced by the various writers who have entered this debate. The first maintains that a great deal of peyote cermonialism was borrowed directly from mescalbean medicine society ceremonialism and that the consumption of both mescalbeans and peyote in ceremonies performed during the early reservation period indicates that these ceremonies were transitional between mescalbean medicine society ceremonies and the ceremonies of the Peyote Religion. This position, put forth and defended by James Howard (1957, 1960, 1962) maintains that contemporary Peyote Religion ceremonialism is to a great extent a direct lineal descendant of mescalbean medicine society ceremonialism. In contrast, La Barre (1957) and Troike (1962) believe that although the use of mescalbeans in the pre-reservation period as a psychotropic substance may have "paved the way" for the reservation use of the hallucinogenic peyote, peyote ceremonialism was little influenced by mescalbean medicine society ceremonialism.

The third position, set forth by Jones and Merrill (n.d.), holds that the use of mescalbeans and the ceremonialism associated with the mescalbean medicine societies had little or no effect on either the acceptance of peyote or the content of Peyote ceremonialism.

The evidence brought together in this report does not support any one of these three positions to the total exclusion of the others, though I believe that in general the data support the position maintained by Professor Jones and myself. Nothing completely unequivocal regarding the relative merits of these positions can be said at present for two reasons: (1) the general origins of the Peyote Religion are obscure and may in fact never be known, though La Barre (1969) and Stewart (1974) have attempted admirably to deal with the problem; and (2) the specific relationships between peyote ceremonialism and mescalbean medicine society ceremonialism have not been investigated for each of the groups who had both, rendering it necessary to speak in generalities rather than specifics. With these qualifications in mind, we can turn to the evidence.

The American Indian groups who have employed mescalbeans at some point in their past can be divided into four categories according to certain aspects of the manner and contexts in which they used mescalbeans. These four categories and the groups assigned to each are as follows:

(1) Groups who employed mescalbeans almost exclusively as items of material culture and are not known ever to have consumed mescalbeans in ritual contexts or to have maintained a mescalbean medicine society. Included here are the Shawnee, Delaware, Kickapoo, Sac, Fox, Ojibwa, Winnebago, Dakota Sioux, Kiowa-Apache, Jicarilla Apache, Western Apache, Santa Clara

Tewa, the Tiwa-speaking residents of Taos Pueblo, the Shoshone, Arapaho, Cheyenne, and Blackfoot.

(2) Groups who consumed mescalbeans but only irregularly or informally. This category includes the Mescalero, Chiricahua, and Lipan Apaches, the Kiowa, and perhaps the Comanche.

(3) Groups who consumed mescalbeans in the context of ceremonies other than those associated with a mescalbean medicine society. The Coahuilteco, Tonkawa, Hasinai Caddo, Prairie Potawatomi, and perhaps some of the Comanche bands can be incorporated into this category.

(4) Groups who consumed mescalbeans in the context of mescalbean medicine society ceremonies or who maintained a mescalbean medicine society without consuming mescalbeans. Included here are the Wichita, Pawnee, Iowa, Oto, Omaha, Ponca, Missouri, Osage, and probably the Kansa.

The American Indian groups who have been involved in the Peyote Religion also can be arranged into four categories, according to the nature of their role in the development and dissemination of the Peyote Religion (La Barre 1969; Stewart 1974). These categories are:

(1) Groups who are considered to have been responsible for the original codification and diffusion of what La Barre (1969) terms the "standard peyote rite." Included here are northeastern Mexico-southern Texas groups like the Carrizo, together with the Tonkawa, and the Lipan and Mescalero Apaches.

(2) Groups who were the principal disseminators of the standard peyote rite. The most prominent members of this category are Comanche and Kiowa followed by the Cheyenne and Arapaho.

(3) Groups who developed and disseminated "non-standard" peyote rites. Principal among these are the Caddo and the Oto.

(4) Groups who primarily were recipients rather than developers or disseminators of one form or another of the Peyote Religion. Included here are the majority of Prairie groups, the Plains and Southwestern groups who were familiar with mescalbeans but are not included in any of the previous three peytoe categories, the Shoshone, and a number of groups, like the Seneca, Cherokee, and Paiute, who received the Peyote Religion but are not known to have previously employed mescalbeans.

A comparison of these two sets of categories provides the means for evaluating the nature and extent of the influence of the use of and ceremonialism associated with mescalbeans during the pre-reservation period on the use of and ceremonialism associated with peyote in the reservation period. All the groups involved in the initial development and diffusion of the standard peyote rite (peyote category 1) also were familiar with mescalbeans and are included in mescalbean categories 2 and 3. (The consumption of mescalbeans by the Carrizo is assumed on the basis of information derived from neighboring and related Coahuiltecan groups in southern Texas [Troike 1962:954-55]). None of these groups maintained a mescalbean medicine society. Some of them are reported to have consumed both mescalbeans and peyote but there is no indication that any of these groups were familiar with or employed mescalbeans prior to peyote. Nor is there any evidence that any aspects of the ceremonialism that some of these groups associated with the consumption of mescalbeans was incorporated into the standard peyote rite.

The principal disseminators of the standard peyote rite (peyote category 2) employed mescalbeans as seed beads probably before they received the Peyote Religion. None of these groups possessed a medicine society in any way comparable to the mescalbean medicine society. A few Kiowa and Comanche individuals may have ingested mescalbeans on occasion and some of the Comanche bands possibly consumed an emetic mescalbean decoction in the context of their green corn ceremonies. There are no reports that the Arapaho and Cheyenne ever consumed mescalbeans. These four groups are included in mescalbean categories 1, 2, and possibly 3. There is no reason to believe that their use of mescalbeans as seed beads would have facilitated their acceptance of peyote, though the Comanche and Kiowa may have been aware of the pharmacologic activity of psychotropic plants through their familiarity with mescalbeans. The absence of mescalbean medicine societies among these groups precludes the possibility that the cermonialism associated with this medicine society would have influenced the content of the peyote ceremonialism that they maintained and diffused.

In addition to the groups responsible for developing and disseminating the standard peyote rite, several groups developed and diffused what, for simplicity's sake, can be termed "non-standard" peyote rites. Pincipal among these groups (included in peyote category 3) are the Caddo and Oto. The Hasinai Caddo can be incorporated into mescalbean category 3. They are reported to have consumed both mescalbeans and peyote in the context of communal ceremonies during the early contact period (Swanton 1942:267). While their use of mescalbeans and peyote in these contexts predated by more than 150 years their acceptance of the Peyote Religion, it is impossible to state that they were aware of and consumed mescalbeans prior to peyote. Though the evidence is suggestive (Troike 1962:949-51). there is no firm indication that any of the Caddo groups maintained a medicine society comparable to the mescalbean medicine societies of the Prairie groups.

The distinctive form of the Peyote Religion associated with the Caddo was formulated and disseminated principally by John Wilson, an individual of Delaware, French, and Caddoan extraction whose primary cultural affiliation was with the Caddo (La Barre 1969:151-61). Wilson employed both mescalbeans and peyote in a ceremony performed during his transitional period between the earlier Ghost Dance and more traditional Indian religions and the later Peyote Religion. The ultimate origins of the manner in which Wilson employed mescalbeans are obscured because he maintained contacts among a number of different Indian groups. However, there is no evidence that he was ever a member of a mescalbean medicine society or that mescalbean medicine society ceremonialism influenced his version of the Peyote Religion. In addition, there is no indication that he was familiar with or ever consumed mescalbeans prior to peyote.

A better case for the direct influence of mescalbean medicine society ceremonialism on peyote ceremonialism can be made for the Oto. The Oto consumed mescalbeans during their mescalbean medicine society ceremonies in pre-reservation times and therefore are included in mescalbean category 4. The earliest form of the Peyote Religion found among the Oto was the standard peyote rite, reportedly introduced by the Tonkawa around 1876 (La Barre 1969:117). There is no evidence that this peyote rite was in any way influenced by the ceremonialism associated with the Oto mescalbean medicine society. On the other hand, Howard (1957:81) reports that the Oto ingested both mescalbeans and peyote in a peyote ceremony held in the early twentieth century. Since the Tonkawa also are reported to have consumed a tea brewed from both peyote and mescalbeans during peyote meetings (Howard 1957:84), the Oto may have adopted this practice from the Tonkawa when they introduced the standard peyote rite. Thus, it is possible that the standard peyote rite taught to the Oto by the Tonkawa was influenced by Tonkawa mescalbean ceremonialism. However, the Tonkawa mescalbean ceremony as described by Gatschet (1884:82) was not performed by the members of a mescalbean medicine society but communally by both men and women in an apparently public setting. The absence of a mescalbean medicine society among the Tonkawa precludes the possibility that the mescalbean ceremonialism that may have influenced their peyote rite was associated with the activities of a mescalbean medicine society.

In any case, the peyote rite for which the Oto are noted is not the standard peyote rite but a Christianized version developed in large part by the Oto Jonathan Koshiway (La Barre 1969:167-69). Koshiway was strongly influenced by the teachings of certain Christian sects and was at one time an Indian evangelist for the Church of Latter-Day Saints. In addition to this Christian influence, his version of the peyote ceremony presumably developed at least partially out of the Oto's standard peyote rite as introduced by the Tonkawa and perhaps influenced by Tonkawa mescalbean ceremonialism. Other than this tenuous connection with mescalbean ceremonialism and the temporal priority of the mescalbean medicine society among the Oto, there is no indication that Koshiway or the Christianized version of the Peyote Religion he supported was in any way influenced by the ceremonialism associated with either the Tonkawa use of mescalbeans or the Oto mescalbean medicine society.

The remaining Indian groups who have practiced the Peyote Religion are classified in peyote category 4 as recipients of the Peyote Religion. Some of these groups may have modified the version of the Peyote Religion they adopted and may have been involved in some proselytizing, but they were not important innovators or disseminators of the Peyote Religion. Groups that fit this characterization and also employed mescalbeans include Plains groups like the Blackfoot and Dakota Sioux, the Shoshone, and the majority of the Prairie groups. These Plains groups along with the Shoshone probably were familiar with mescalbeans before learning of peyote, but they employed mescalbeans solely as items of material culture. They are included in mescalbean category 1. They could have been totally unaware of the psychotropic properties of mescalbeans; if so, their previous familiarity with mescalbeans probably would not have facilitated their acceptance of peyote.

Several of the Prairie groups can also be included in mescalbean category 1 since they used mescalbeans exclusively as items of material culture. Their reaction to the introduction of the Peyote Religion and any modifications they may have introduced into the version they practiced presumably was not influenced by their previous use of mescalbeans. The

Prairie Potawatomi consumed mescalbeans in the context of a ceremony that may be a highly modified version of the mescalbean medicine society ceremonies of one of the Prairie groups but are included here in mescalbean category 3. The remaining Prairie groups maintained mescalbean medicine societies and most are either known or presumed to have consumed mescalbeans in the context of the ceremonies associated with this medicine society. These groups, then, are incorporated into mescalbean category 4.

The Prairie groups who maintained mescalbean medicine societies may have accepted peyote more readily because they were familiar with the pyschotropic effects of mescalbeans, but the number of individuals who were allowed to consume mescalbeans among these groups probably was rather small. There is evidence that most if not all the Prairie groups that maintained a mescalbean medicine society restricted the consumption of mescalbeans to society members. While information regarding the psychotropic properties of mescalbeans presumably diffused beyond the boundaries of the medicine society, the majority of individuals within these Prairie groups would have had secondary rather than direct exposure to the pharmacologic action of mescalbeans. Thus, within any of these Prairie groups, the individuals most inclined to accept peyote presumably would have been the members of the mescalbean medicine society. Yet in many cases it was the members of the medicine societies--the "traditionalists"--who were most staunchly and vociferously opposed to the introduction of the Peyote Religion, since it disrupted traditional tribal religious practices. In view of the traditionalists' opposition to the

Peyote Religion, the restricted use of mescalbeans among the Prairie groups, and the fact that most of these groups received rather than developed or diffused the Peyote Religion, it seems unlikely that the prior presence of mescalbeans among these groups would have influenced to any great degree their reaction to the Peyote Religion. Nor is it likely that the ceremonialism associated with their mescalbean medicine societies would have altered the form or content of the peyote ceremonies these groups performed.

The evidence presented in this overview has failed to provide support either for the proposition that (1) the ceremonialism associated with the pre-reservation mescalbean medicine societies had a direct and substantial impact on the ceremonialism of the reservation Peyote Religion or for the proposition that (2) a familiarity with mescalbeans in the pre-reservation period enhanced the diffusion of peyotism in the reservation period. However, neither of these propositions can be rejected out of hand because the evidence presently available--both published and preserved in museum collections--is sufficiently adequate to stimulate speculation about such problems but inadequate to resolve them completely. The second of the two propositions is the more probable if only because it is weaker, proposing only general rather than specific influence. Since the Peyote rite was codified in northern Mexico and adjacent portions of the United States and the mescalbean medicine societies were restricted to the Prairie area, there is no reason to believe that the ceremonialism associated with the latter could have had a significant input into the former. Yet this does not preclude the possibility that mescalbean medicine society ceremonialism could have had more local influence on the peyote ceremonialism of groups who maintained this medicine society in pre-reservation times.

A museum specimen of Pawnee provenience (Specimen 67) discovered during this investigation suggests that the mescalbean medicine society ceremonialism of the Pawnee may have had some impact on their peyote ceremonialism. A single peyote button was found in direct association with the paraphernalia of the Pawnee mescalbean medicine society. The peyote button is wrapped in a strip of buckskin and placed in the bottom of a turtle paw bag, which also contains a mescalbean, a plum pit die, and a portion of a deer's tail (see Fig. 19). This bag was included in the general medicine bundle of the Pawnee mescalbean medicine society. The significance of this specimen is difficult to evaluate. Though the bundle was collected sometime around 1915 and is wrapped in an American flag bearing 48 stars, it is impossible to tell if the peyote button was added before or after the introduction of the Peyote Religion among the Pawnee. Perhaps the Pawnee, like the Wichita and Shawnee (La Barre 1969:26, 120), included peyote buttons in their bundles long before they received the organized Peyote Religion. In any case, while this specimen may suggest that Pawnee mescalbean ceremonialism influenced Pawnee peyote ceremonialism, it can likewise be interpreted as an indication that Pawnee peyotism influenced their mescalbean medicine society during the last year of its existence.

Surprisingly, very few of the museum specimens of mescalbeans examined were explicitly associated with the paraphernalia of the Peyote

Religion. Of course, the prominent place of mescalbeans in Peyote paraphernalia is unquestionably established in the published literature (La Barre 1969; Schultes 1937), but the evidence collected during the present investigation indicates that American Indian groups who have had access to mescalbeans have employed them for a wide range of purposes independent of their use of peyote both prior to and following their development or receipt of the Peyote Religion.

I believe that mescalbeans are present in the paraphernalia of the Peyote Religion because they are just one of many traditional items that were incorporated into the Peyote Religion complex. It is possible that some of the groups who were responsible for developing and diffusing the Peyote Religion in its pristine form introduced mescalbeans into Peyote paraphernalia. At least some of these groups may have employed both mescalbeans and peyote in the same ceremonies prior to the formulation of the Peyote Religion and may have maintained some symbolic associations between the two plants. If these groups did not introduce mescalbeans into Peyote paraphernalia, it is likely that the Comanche and Kiowa did because they employed mescalbeans as items of material culture before they began their intensive proselytizing of the Peyote Religion.

IV. DESCRIPTION OF SPECIMENS

In the following pages, I will describe in detail all the archaeological and ethnographic specimens of mescalbeans of which I am aware, together with a few specimens of Erythrina flabelliformis. I have drawn on both published and unpublished sources of information in compiling these descriptions; the source of information for each specimen is indicated in its description. For convenience, the specimen descriptions are arranged in alphabetical order by ethnic group. Specimens associated with subgroups of a larger ethnic category are included in the alphabetical position of the general category; e.g., Mescalero Apache specimens are described in conjunction with other Apache specimens rather than after the Mandan.

A number of these museum specimens include substances of animal or plant origins (i.e., feathers, claws, hooves, seeds, roots, etc.) or inorganic materials like rocks and powdered earth. In some cases I have attempted to identify these materials, but, except for specimens of Sophora secundiflora, Erythrina flabelliformis, Abrus precatorius, and Lophophora williamsii, my identifications should be considered tentative.

The descriptions of the mescalbean specimens associated with each American Indian group are prefaced by a brief overview of the manner in which the group employed mescalbeans. These synopses are supplemented by references to the use of mescalbeans as items of material culture by the group or groups in question in ways not documented by the museum specimens. These overviews are not intended to list every purpose for which a group employed mescalbeans but are designed to enable the reader to view the more material uses of mescalbeans in a broader perspective.

The museum collections visited during the investigation were searched as thoroughly as possible in the limited time available but in most cases large portions of these collections remain unexamined. The sections of the collections that were examined in each of the museums visited are as follows:

(1) American Museum of Natural History: portions of the Plains and Southwest collections; (2) Dayton Museum of Natural History: the entire ethnographic collection was surveyed by J. M. Heilman, Curator of Anthropology; (3) Museum of the American Indian, Heye Foundation: only those specimens that were requested; (4) National Museum of Natural History, Smithsonian Institution: Northeast, Plains, Southwest (except pottery, basketry, and Navajo blankets), Basin and Plateau; (5) Peabody Museum of Archaeology and Ethnology, Harvard University: Plains only; (6) Peabody Museum of Natural History, Yale University: Northeast Plains, Southwest, Basin, and Plateau; (7) University Museum, University of Pennsylvania: Plains, Southwest, Basin, Plateau, and portions of the Northeast.

All the groups known to have employed mescalbeans at some time are listed below in the order in which their use of mescalbeans will be described.

1. Prehistoric Southwestern Texas
2. Apache
   a. Lipan Apache
   b. Jicarilla Apache
   c. Chiricahua Apache
   d. Mescalero Apache
   e. Western Apache
   f. White Mountain Apache
3. Arapaho
4. Arikara
5. Blackfoot
6. Caddo
7. Cheyenne
   a. Northern Cheyenne
   b. Southern Cheyenne
8. Coahuilteco
9. Comanche
10. Crow
11. Delaware
12. Hidatsa
13. Iowa
14. Kansa
15. Kickapoo
16. Kiowa
17. Kiowa-Apache
18. Mandan
19. Missouri
20. Ojibwa
21. Omaha
22. Osage
23. Oto
24. Pawnee
25. Ponca
26. Prairie Potawatomi
27. Pueblos
   a. Santa Clara
   b. Taos
28. Sac and Fox
29. Shawnee
30. Shoshone and Northern Ute
31. Sioux
   a. Santee
   b. Brule
   c. Yankton
   d. Teton
   e. Oglala
   f. Upper Yanktonai
32. Tonkawa
33. Wichita
34. Winnebago
35. Unidentified

ARCHAEOLOGICAL SPECIMENS

To my knowledge, no mescalbeans have been recovered from prehistorically or historically inhabited archaeological sites outside the area where mescalbeans occur naturally. To date, mescalbeans have been recovered from thirteen caves and rockshelters in southwestern Texas, two caves in the northern Mexican state of Coahuila, and a rockshelter in southwestern New Mexico. All these sites are located within the natural range of Sophora secundiflora (see Fig. 4). Cultural deposits which have yielded mescalbeans range in age from circa 8000 B.P. to the historical period. With two exceptions, none of the mescalbeans recovered from these

Figure 5a. Buckskin loincloth recovered from Murrah Cave in Val Verde County, Texas. Three longitudinally split mescalbeans are attached to its fringe. Reproduced courtesy of The Museum, Texas Tech University.

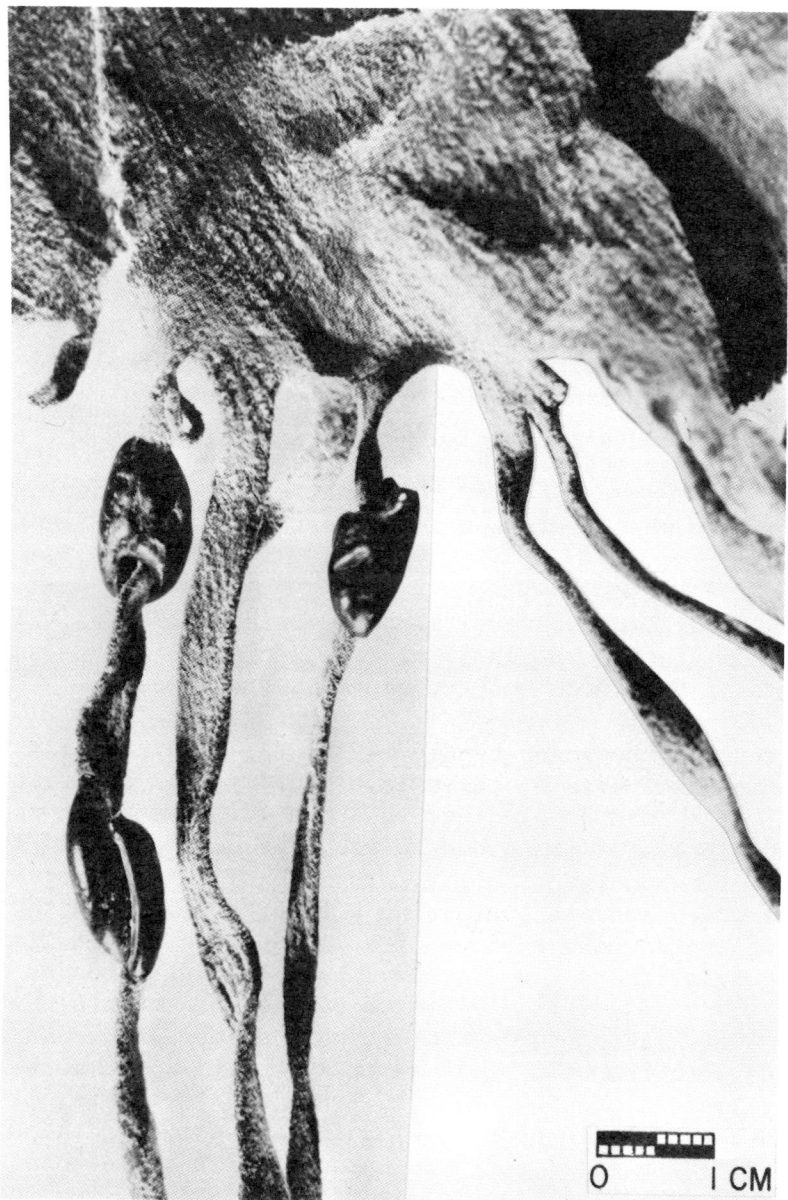

Figure 5b. An enlarged view of the same specimen, revealing the method of attachment and the distinctive hilum of Sophora secundiflora. Reproduced courtesy of The Museum, Texas Tech University.

sites display evidence of having been preferentially treated by humans (Jones and Merrill n.d.). The two exceptions to this generalization are described below.

Prehistoric Southwestern Texas

Specimen 1: A buckskin loincloth, 45 cm long (excluding fringe) and 27 cm wide at the top, was found neatly folded on top of a bundle of Mormon tea (Ephedra sp.) with seven pieces of red paint placed on top of it (Fig. 5). A deeply fringed buckskin strip is sewn to the bottom of the loincloth. Three longitudinally split mescalbeans are attached to two of the fringes, one mescalbean on one fringe, two on the other. No definite date can be supplied for this specimen, but the cultural deposits of the cave from which this specimen was recovered are classified as Archaic.

The Museum, Texas Tech University. W.C. Holden (1937:65, Plate 11A) recovered this specimen in 1937, fifteen inches below the surface of Murrah Cave, in Val Verde County, southwestern Texas.

Specimen 2: "Medicine bundle" (Fig. 6). A diagonally twined basket or bag was found covered by three layers of matting and resting upon a woven rabbit fur robe or blanket, which in turn rested upon a layer of matting and a bunch of grass and twigs. The bag contained the following items: (1) two bundles of heavy cord made of twisted vegetal fibers, (2) a small woven package containing a flint or chert knife, two bundles of sinew (one bound with a piece of split Spanish dagger leaf, the other with lechuguilla fibers), and a small ball of pinkish paint clay; (3) a buckskin thong; (4) what appears to be a flint knapping kit, consisting of three antler flaking tools, cut or worn at each end, and a small piece of deer hide with the hair still adhering to it; (5) a mussel shell; (6) three flint leaf-shaped blades, five crude side scrapers, five unworked flints, and a projectile point; (7) a flattened mano perhaps used as a hammer stone; (8) a small terrapin carapace with holes bored along its circumference; (9) eleven jackrabbit mandible halves, ten left halves and one right half; (10) three pieces of red paint stone; (11) thirty-eight mescalbeans; and (12) one hundred and eighty-seven Texas buckeyes (Ungnadia speciosa). This specimen, along with the cultural deposits with which it was associated, is classified as Archaic; no specific date has been assigned to it.

Texas Archeological Research Laboratory, University of Texas at Austin, catalogue numbers 440-483, 493. This specimen was recovered by A. M. Woolsey in 1936 from the deposits of one of the Horseshoe Ranch Caves at a depth of thirteen inches. These caves are located in Val Verde County,

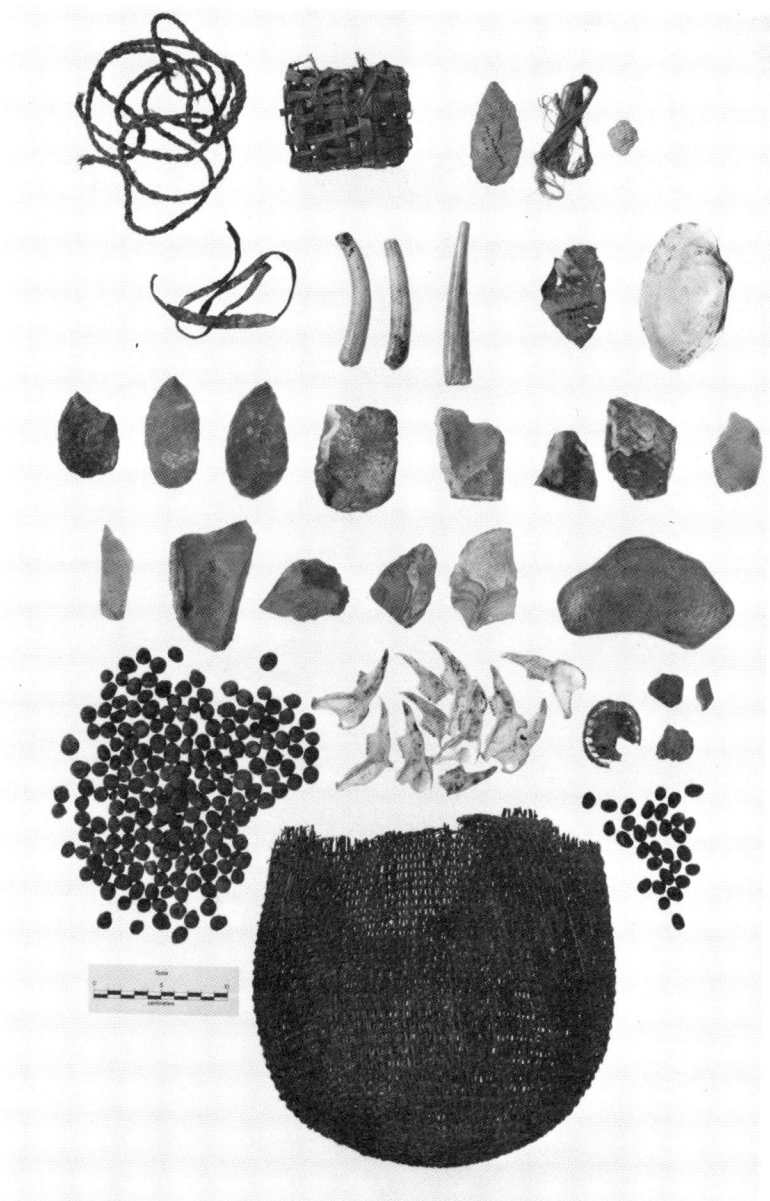

Figure 6. Contents of the "medicine bundle" recovered from the Horseshoe Ranch Caves in Val Verde County, Texas. The seeds to the right of the twined bag are mescalbeans while those to the left are Texas buckeyes. Reproduced courtesy of the Texas Archeological Research Laboratory, The University of Texas at Austin.

southwestern Texas, just to the north of the Rio Grande River and to the east of the Pecos River (Woolsey 1936; Butler 1948).

ETHNOGRAPHIC SPECIMENS

Apache

Castetter and Opler (1936:54, 61) report that the Chiricahua and Mescalero Apaches occasionally mixed mescalbeans with their corn beer in the past, but there is no substantial evidence that any of the Apachean groups traditionally consumed mescalbeans on a regular basis or in a ritual setting. Voegelin (see Howard 1957:76-77) learned from Delaware informants in 1939 that the "Apache" (no group specified but apparently one located in Oklahoma) formerly consumed mescalbeans in a ceremonial context to induce an intoxicated state. In addition, there are several Coyote myths collected among Lipan, Chiricahua, and Mescalero Apaches that describe how the Coyote Trickster hoodwinked a group of unsuspecting travellers into consuming a decoction of mescalbeans (Opler 1940:164-65, 190; Opler 1942:48-49; Castetter and Opler 1936:54). These myths indicate that at least some Apachean groups were familiar with the procedures for preparing mescalbeans for consumption even though they may not have done so. In general, modern Apache groups--including the Mescalero, Chiricahua, Lipan, Jicarilla, and Western Apaches--appear to employ mescalbeans almost exclusively as seed beads, though the Lipan also apply the ground up seeds mixed with fat to their hair to kill lice (Castetter and Opler 1936:54; Opler 1976: personal communication). In addition to the specimens described below, I discovered several photographs in the collections of the National Anthropological Archives, Smithsonian

Institution, that depict Chiricahua Apache women of the Warm Springs and Cochise bands wearing necklaces prepared at least in part from seeds that resemble those of Sophora secundiflora and Erythrina flabelliformis (negative numbers 2520-A & B; 2523-A & B; and 2580-B-6).

Specimen 3: <u>Man's tanned and fringed buckskin leggings</u>. The leggings are stained a yellow color and are cut into fringes along the sides and bottom. A series of tanned leather thongs are looped through the leggings to taper them. These strings are arranged into several groups, four on the right legging and six on the left. On one side of the leggings these thongs have two loose ends, to which are attached a variety of objects. From the top of the right legging, the attachments to each group of strings are as follows: first group: nothing attached; second group: a pink cloth medicine packet containing an unidentified material; third group, consisting of ten separate ends: no attachments appear on the third, fifth, seventh, and tenth ends while a shell is attached to the first end, a silver metal bead followed by a mescalbean is strung on the second and the fourth, a mescalbean appears on the sixth and eighth, and a green "pinked" ribbon is tied to the ninth. On the fourth and final group of strings, the ends bear in order the following attachments: a mescalbean, nothing, a metal bead followed by a mescalbean, a "pinked" red ribbon, a metal bead, and a piece of unidentified fur. On the left legging, there are no attachments on the end of the thongs of the first three groups. The fourth group bears one green "pinked" ribbon, two mescalbeans on separate strings, and one red "pinked" ribbon. The fifth group exhibits, on the six ends of three separate strings, three mescalbeans preceded by two silver metal beads, two mescalbeans with one metal bead each, one red "pinked" ribbon, and an unidentified piece of fur. The sixth group displays one red "pinked" ribbon and four mescalbeans on separate strings. There are eight mescalbeans on the right legging and eleven on the left, making a total of nineteen on this specimen. The seeds are of a uniform, very dark maroon color. They apparently have been perforated with a hot drill, but the dark color of the seeds obscures most evidences of the discoloration that results from the use of this method of perforation. The mescalbeans are of medium size, all being approximately 1.2 cm wide and ranging from 1.1 to 1.4 cm in length.

University Museum, University of Pennsylvania, catalogue number L-84-1841 a-b. Collected by A. H. Gottschall near Dulce Lake, New Mexico. No collection date given; the Academy of Natural Sciences of Philadelphia received it in May, 1914. Lent to the University Museum by the Academy of Natural Sciences in 1937.

Specimen 4: <u>Chiricahua Apache saddlebag</u>. This specimen was on exhibit at the time of investigation, and a complete description of it was impossible to complete. In general, it is a tanned leather bag of the parfleche type. The front of the bag bears a red felt strip that serves as a background for leather cut-outs. In the center of the bag is a row of beads consisting of alternating stripes of blue and gold. Long fringes are attached to the bottom of the bag and five seeds are strung on these fringes about three-quarters of the distance from where the fringe begins. Of these seeds, all of which are deep maroon in color, only one can be identified with any certainty as Erythrina flabelliformis. The remaining four seeds are very similar in color and shape to the identifiable seed, suggesting that they, too, are E. flabelliformis. However, they could equally be the seeds of Sophora secundiflora since their seed scars are obscured from view.

Museum of the American Indian (Heye Foundation), catalogue number 2/1199. Collected by M. R. Harrington near Lawton, Oklahoma, circa 1909. Accession date: 1909.

Specimen 5: Mescalero Apache mescalbean necklace. This necklace consists of fifty-seven perforated mescalbeans strung on double threads. It is believed to have been manufactured for sale, with no additional significance attached to it. Information on this specimen was supplied by Dr. Bernard L. Fontana.

Arizona State Museum, University of Arizona, catalogue number E-3293. Donated by Tom Bahti who acquired it in Gallup, New Mexico, in 1956 or 1957.

Specimen 6: Western Apache charm from Whiteriver, Arizona. This specimen consists of several strings of red, white, blue, and yellow glass trade beads wrapped around what appears to be a single mescalbean. The identification of this seed as Sophora secundiflora is strengthened by the fact that two seed pods of this plant were collected at the same time and place as the charm. The seed is supposed to promote good health for the owner and to crack if someone is telling a lie about the owner or if a witch is in the neighborhood. I have not examined this specimen; the description presented here is based on a photograph and information supplied by Dr. Bernard L. Fontana.

Arizona State Museum, University of Arizona, catalogue number 74-61-1. Collected by Mrs. E. E. Guenther of Whiteriver, Arizona, and donated to the museum in November 1974.

Specimen 7: White Mountain Apache "charm against witchcraft." This specimen is composed of a tanned white buckskin thong wrapped around two seeds. Although portions of the seeds are visible through perforations in the thong, a definite identification of them cannot be made. Given their shape and maroon color, it is likely that they are either mescalbeans or coralbeans. I have not seen this specimen; I have relied on information and a photograph provided by Dr. Bernard L. Fontana for my description of it.

Arizona State Museum, University of Arizona, catalogue number 21404. Collected by Grenville Goodwin at Bylas, Arizona, and donated to the museum on March 4, 1936.

Arapaho

In 1820, Thomas Say (in James 1905, vol. 16:216-17) discovered that an Arapaho shaman had included among the contents of his personal medicine bundle what appear to have been mescalbeans and perhaps the seeds of Erythrina flabelliformis. There is no additional published information regarding Arapaho use of mescalbeans and no indication that they ever consumed mescalbeans.

Specimen 8: Man's tanned buckskin leggings (see Fig. 7), 91 cm long, 51 cm wide at the top and bottom (measurements include the fringe). Strips of blue cloth, sewn to the interior of the top of each legging, apparently were formerly employed to attach the leggings to a belt; they are now torn off even with the top of the leggings. The leggings are fully fringed along the edges and bottom. A series of leather strings are looped through the leggings about 5 cm from the fringe to taper them. This series of strings extends for about two-thirds of the length of the leggings, beginning at the edge of the bottom fringe. Mescalbeans (total = forty-eight), silver metal beads (total = four), strips of fur, possibly a deer tail (total = five), and, on one legging, a shell is attached to these strings. The leggings are yellowish tan in color but are dyed a medium brown between the strings and the fringe. The fringe is dyed a deep green color opposite the series of strings while the remainder of the fringe is light brown. Painted decorations appear on each legging on the side of the strings opposite the fringe. On one legging, the painted design consists of two sets of five lines each (blue line, green line, red line, green line, and blue line) and one set of four lines (blue line, green line, space, green line, blue line). The three sets of lines are spaced at even intervals paralleling the series of strings. The other legging has three sets of green dots instead of lines; these dots are arranged in horizontal rows with four rows of dots per set. These three sets also are evenly spaced on the legging. A strip of trade beads runs along the fringe on the opposite side of the leggings. This beaded strip continues along the base of each legging above the bottom fringe in two parallel rows. The portion of the legging between these two rows is dyed a medium brown color. A total of forty-eight mescalbeans are

74

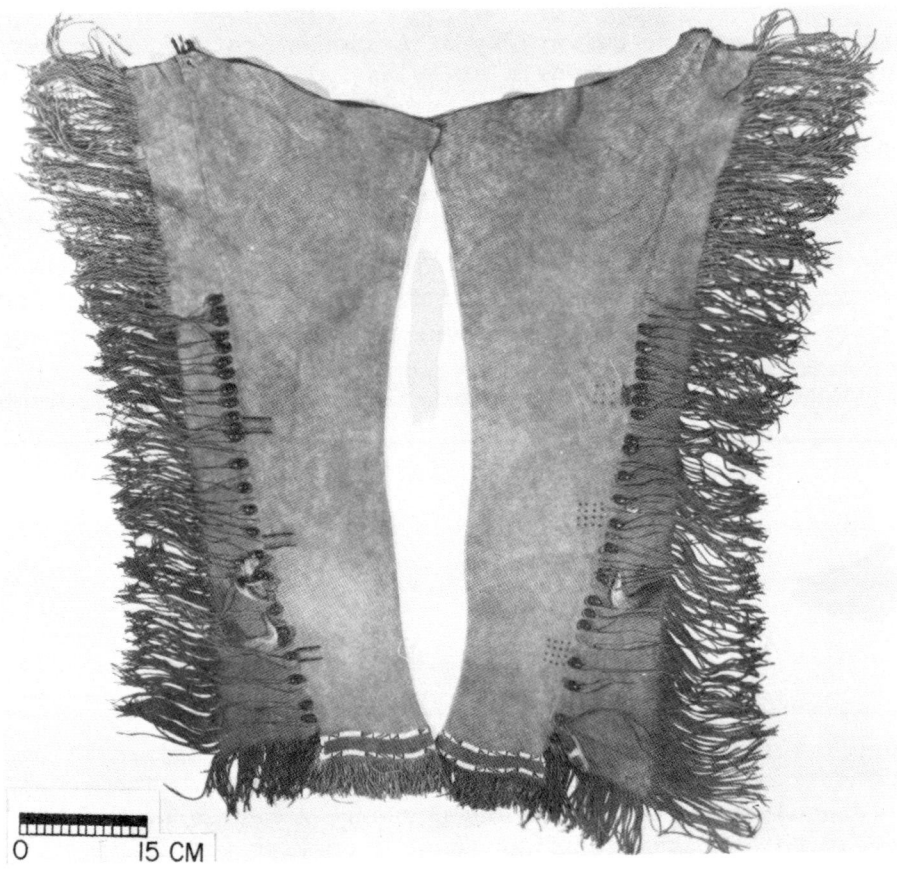

Figure 7a. Specimen 8: A pair of Arapaho leggings, with mescalbeans strung on the leather thongs that serve to taper the leggings. Smithsonian Institution, catalogue number 165823.

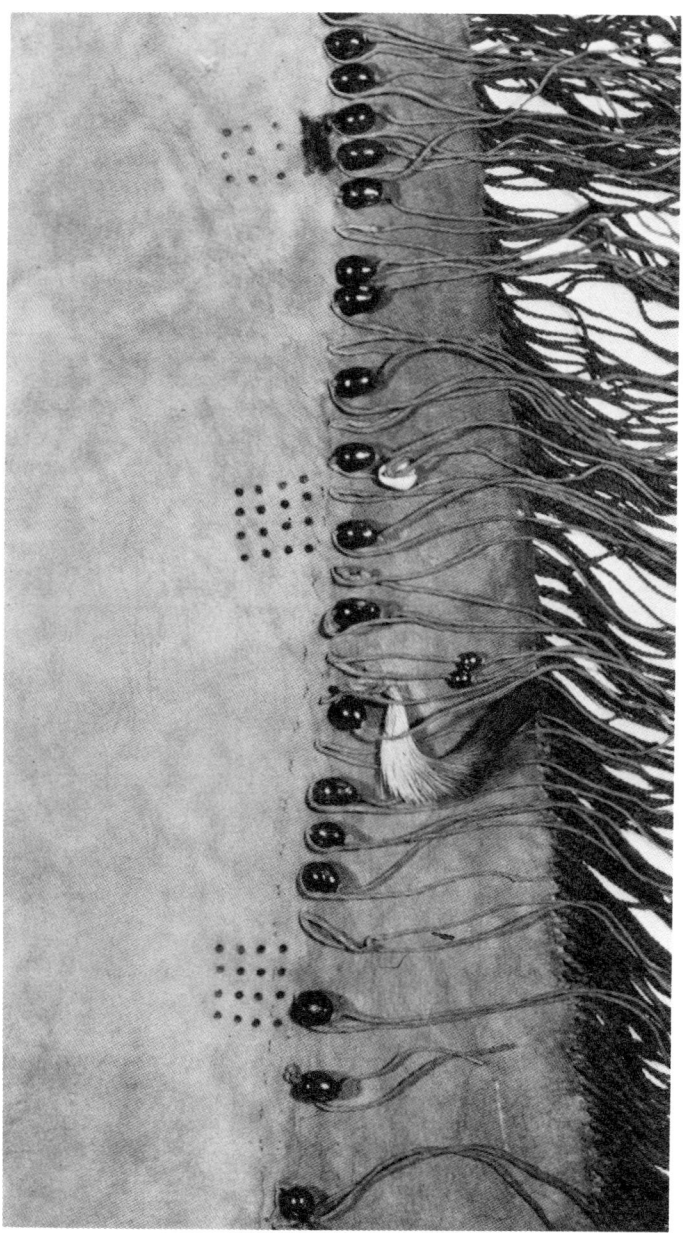

Figure 7b. An enlarged view of the same specimen.

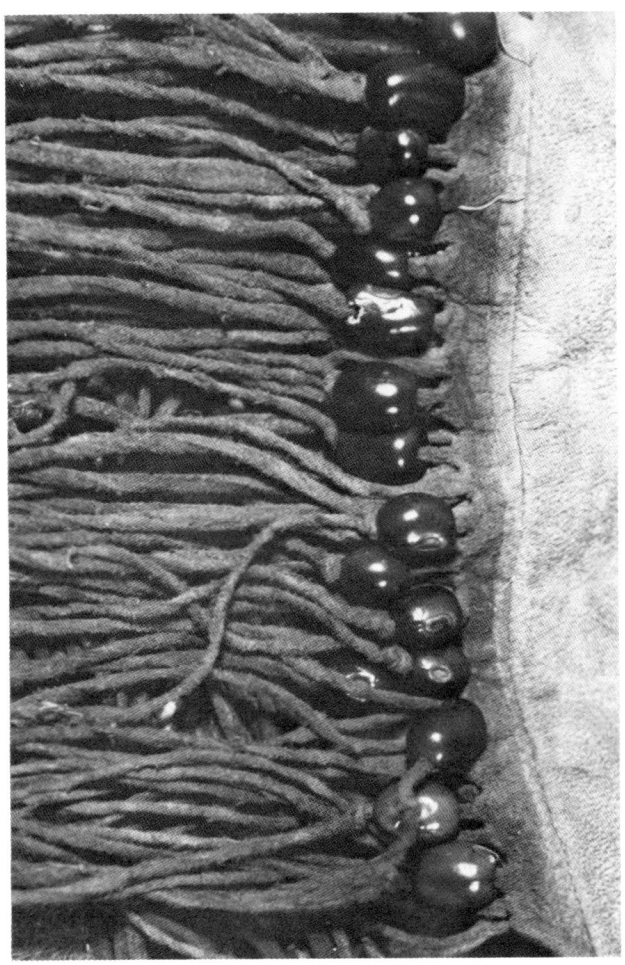

Figure 8. Specimen 11: Mescalbeans and coralbeans juxtaposed on the sleeve fringe of an Arapaho shirt. The sixth, ninth, and eleventh seeds from the top clearly are coralbeans, while the twelfth is a mescalbean. University Museum, University of Pennsylvania, catalogue number 31-23-123.

attached to these leggings, twenty-six to one legging, twenty-two to the other. All the mescalbeans are deep maroon in color and all seem to have been perforated with a hot drill. They are rather large in size ranging from 1.2 to 1.8 cm long and 1.0 to 1.5 cm wide.

Smithsonian Institution, catalogue number 165823, accession number 26674. Collected by H. R. Voth; no collection date or locality given. Acquired by purchase. Accession date: February 9, 1893.

Specimen 9: <u>Man's tanned and fringed leggings</u>, with a concave cut at top and a leather strip looped at the top of each legging for attachment to a belt. The leggings are 95 cm long at their longest point and 80 cm long at the shortest (including fringe). They are 32 cm wide at the bottom and 42 cm wide at the top (including fringe). A row of looped rawhide strings tapers the leggings. Faint traces of two red lines with a blue line in between are found between some of these strings. To the interior of these strings, the leggings are yellowish brown with some traces of green dye; to the exterior, between the seam and the side fringe, the leggings are dyed a dark green. The side fringe consists of a series of paired and twisted leather thongs, also dyed green, and the bottom edge of the leggings have been cut into short square fringes. A beaded strip--composed of dark blue, light blue, and red trade beads arranged in diagonal lines on a white beaded background--extends along the side and bottom fringe of one side of each legging. Parallel rows of these beads are sewn along the bottom of the reverse side of the leggings, between which the leggings are dyed a reddish brown color. Mescalbeans are attached to several of the loose ends of the strings which serve to taper the leggings. On the right legging, there are twenty-two pairs of these ends. The first seven pairs from the top of the legging have no attachments. The eighth pair bears a single mescalbean on one of its loose ends, the ninth pair is without mescalbeans, the tenth pair bears one mescalbean on each of its ends and then every alternate pair bears a mescalbean on each of its ends. There are a total of fourteen mescalbeans on the right legging. The pattern is more or less identical on the left legging, except that the ninth pair of ends from the top of the legging are the first to bear mescalbeans and there are twenty-three pairs of these strings. There are fifteen mescalbeans on the left legging, bringing the total number of mescalbeans on the pair of leggings to twenty-nine. There are no mescalbeans on the reverse side of the leggings. The mescalbeans are all of a deep maroon color and are relatively large, ranging from 1.5 to 1.7 cm in length and 1.0 to 1.5 cm in width. Most of the mescalbeans present apparently were perforated with a cold drill, but some exhibit signs of burning and the ends of others have been cut off to provide larger perforations for attachment to the strings.

University Museum, University of Pennsylvania, catalogue number 31-23-122. Collected by George H. Starr, apparently at the Darlington Agency in Oklahoma. No collection date given. Purchased from George E. Starr in 1931.

Specimen 10: <u>Arapaho (?) loincloth</u>. No measurements were made of this specimen. It consists of a strip of red cloth with two pieces of fringed buckskin sewn on top. The two buckskin pieces cover almost the entire surface of the piece of cloth, with only a small open space in the middle between them. Each piece of buckskin is beaded in its center with a crescent and star design below which is a beaded and fringed semi-circular design. Next are two rows of geometrical designs done in orange and blue on a white background. The bottom of each side of the breech-cloth is deeply fringed. A rawhide string is attached to each of the two bottom corners of each side upon which are strung alternating pairs of spherical and tubular glass trade beads. On three of the four bottom corners of the breechcloth, these strings are completed with what seems to be a deer dewclaw followed by a single mescalbean and a knot. The fourth string is broken off and contains only two spherical and two tubular trade beads. There are a total of three mescalbeans on this specimen. No measurements were made of them; they all are of a deep maroon color.

Dayton Museum of Natural History, catalogue number A-2399, accession number 3562. No collection date or locality given. According to the accompanying catalogue information, this specimen was made by "Wongon" for Dr. Corey. J. M. Heilman, Curator of Anthropology at the Dayton Museum, suggests that this specimen, which identified only as "Plains U.S.," is of Arapaho provenience on the basis of general information regarding Dr. Corey's collection.

Specimen 11: <u>Man's tanned and fringed buckskin shirt</u>, 90 cm long with fringe (75.5 cm long without fringe), 55 cm wide at the bottom, 43 cm wide at the top (excluding the sleeves, which are 60 cm long with fringe). Triangular-shaped pieces of buckskin, dyed a reddish-brown color, are sewn to the shirt at the neck. These pieces are deeply fringed, and the fringe is dyed a dark green. Strips of deeply fringed leather, also dyed dark green, are attached to the shirt at the shoulders, in two rows on the underside of the sleeves about at their midpoints, and along the bottom of the shirt. The bottoms of the sleeves have been cut into short, square fringes. A row of buckskin thongs is looped through the shirt across its middle on both the front and back sides. Rows of blue and red trade beads are sewn onto the shirt along the top of the shoulder and the triangular neck pieces. The sleeves and the remainder of the shirt, except the fringes, are a yellowish color with slight traces of green dye. In addition, a series of parallel, light red lines have been drawn vertically on the upper portion of the shirt, front and back. The seeds of both <u>Sophora</u> <u>secundiflora</u> and <u>Erythrina</u> <u>flabelliformis</u> are strung on the fringe of the shoulders and the sleeves (Fig. 8). The maker of this shirt apparently distinguished between the <u>S. secundiflora</u> and <u>E. flabelliformis</u> seeds since they tend to be grouped, but there is no definite pattern in their arrangement. There are no <u>E. flabelliformis</u> seeds on the back row of fringe on the right and left sleeves, on the front or back sides of the right shoulder, or on the front side of the left shoulder; a total of forty-seven mescalbeans appears in these locations. On the front row of fringe on the right sleeve there are nine S. secundiflora seeds and one E. flabelliformis seed. On the front row of the left sleeve there are seven S. secundiflora seeds and nine E. flabelliformis seeds. On the back side of the left shoulder there are two S. secundiflora seeds and seven E. flabelliformis seeds. On the shirt as a whole, there are eighty-eight S. secundiflora seeds and seventeen E. flabelliformis seeds. Both the S. secundiflora and E. flabelliformis seeds are deep maroon in color and the majority apparently have been perforated with a cold drill, though some exhibit slight discoloration and cracking perhaps as a result of the use of a hot drill. The mescalbeans vary somewhat in size, ranging from 0.8 to 1.5 cm long and 0.9 to 1.3 cm wide. The E. flabelliformis seeds are from 0.9 cm to 1.7 cm long and all are approximately 1.0 cm wide.

University Museum, University of Pennsylvania, catalogue number 31-23-123. Collected by George H. Starr, apparently at the Darlington Agency in Oklahoma. No collection date given. Purchased from George E. Starr in 1931.

Specimen 12: Hide painting; no measurements were made of this specimen. The principal decoration on this specimen is a painting which, according to the accompanying catalogue information, depicts the divisions of the tribe. It consists of a rectangle drawn with parallel lines interrupted at intervals with geometrical designs. Within the rectangle appear forty-one human figures and a central design of a crescent and three stars surrounded by a circle of projectile points. Outside the rectangle in one corner an eagle feather with its base wrapped and tied to a leather disk is attached. A comparable leather disk is found in the other corner of the same side of the hide but no feather is attached to it. The edge of the hide is fringed in several places and rawhide thongs are looped through the edge of one side of the hide. A single mescalbean is strung on each of these thongs. A total of thirteen mescalbeans are present on this specimen; no information on their size or color was recorded.

Dayton Museum of Natural History, catalogue number A-2581, accession number 3414. Collected by H. E. Talbott. No collection date or locality given. According to the accompanying catalogue information, this painting was executed by "Rabbit Tail."

Specimen 13: Arapaho (?) buckskin horse draping; no measurements were made of this specimen. It consists of two strips of buckskin tied together with rawhide strings at the top and attached to a squarish piece of buckskin at the bottom center. A row of spherical beads is placed between the central buckskin piece and the two strips. Near the top of each of these strips is attached a circular disk, decorated around its circumference with two rows of metal brads with a smaller disk in its center.

Attached to the top of each of these disks are three buckskin strings on each of which are strung two small tubular beads separated by a large tubular bead. Five similar thongs are looped through the bottom of each of these disks on which are strung small and large tubular beads followed by a mescalbean, three small tubular beads, two small round beads and a shell. Below these disks, the strips and the central buckskin piece are beaded with geometrical and stylized designs on a white background. According to the catalogue information that accompanies this specimen, these designs represent "the powers that govern on and above the earth: Sun, moon, stars, eagle, rivers, mountains, prairies, and buffalo." Along the base of the central piece of buckskin are looped a series of buckskin thongs, each bearing several differently sized spherical glass beads below which the thongs are knotted. Similar thongs are attached to the base of the buckskin strips, but each of these thongs, in addition to the spherical beads, have a single mescalbean strung on them, followed by what seems to be a deer dewclaw, two small tubular beads, and a knot. There are a total of twenty-two mescalbeans on this specimen; no measurements of these mescalbeans were made. They all are of a deep maroon color.

Dayton Museum of Natural History, catalogue number A-2377, accession number 3494. Collected by H. E. Talbott. No collection date or locality are given. The association of this specimen with the Arapaho is suggested by J. M. Heilman, Curator of Anthropology at the Dayton Museum, on the basis of general information regarding the larger collection of which this specimen originally was a part.

Specimen 14: <u>Arapaho (?) or Crow (?) wooden lance</u>, approximately 180 cm long with a steel point approximately 19 cm long. Several parallel rows of metal brads are embedded in the wooden shaft just below the steel point and approximately midway down the shaft. A hole is bored through the shaft between the metal brads and the spearpoint, through which passes a rawhide thong. Three large glass beads are strung on this thong, below which is attached a circular leather disk with metal brads around its circumference and a smaller metal disk in its center. Seven pairs of rawhide strings are looped through the bottom of the leather disk. A single mescalbean is strung on each pair of these strings. No measurements of these mescalbeans were made. They all are rather large, perhaps 1.5 to 1.7 cm long and 1.0 to 1.3 cm wide, and are all of a uniform deep maroon color. With the exception of the central pair, these rawhide strings remain unadorned for the remainder of their length. The central pair bears several large glass beads followed by several rows of small glass trade beads wrapped around the base of a leather strip which serves as a wrapper for a lock of human hair.

Dayton Museum of Natural History, catalogue number A-642, accession number 3411. Collected by H. E. Talbott. No collection date or locality given. This specimen is identified with only "U.S.A." as a provenience.

J. M. Heilman, Curator of Anthropology at the Dayton Museum, suggests, on the basis of general information regarding the collection of which this specimen was a part, that it is of Arapaho or Crow provenience.

Arikara

There is no indication that the Arikara ever employed mescalbeans for any purposes other than as seed beads in bandoleers worn during reservation Peyote Religion ceremonies (Howard n.d.). Howard (1962:125) claims that the Arikara performed, presumably in pre-reservation times, a mescalbean ceremony that they had adopted from the Pawnee. The presence of this ceremony among the Arikara is not otherwise substantiated in any of the published sources dealing specifically with the Arikara. No museum specimens of mescalbeans of Arikara provenience were discovered during the investigation.

Blackfoot

There is no evidence that the Blackfoot employed mescalbeans for any purposes other than as seed beads. Ewers (1945:Fig. 31) pictures a Blackfoot necklace composed of fifty-six seed beads which apparently are mescalbeans. No museum specimens of mescalbeans attributed to the Blackfoot were encountered during this investigation.

Caddo

The Hasinai Caddo are reported in the early eighteenth century to have performed communal dances in which a man or woman consumed either mescalbeans or peyote to induce an intoxicated state apparently accompanied by visions (Hidalgo in Swanton 1942:267). The Hasinai also may have included mescalbeans in psychotropic decoctions consumed for divinatory purposes prior to undertaking raiding expeditions and to initiate young men into the ranks of their shamans (Espinosa in Swanton 1942:284-86). More recently, Parsons (1941:34, 36, 36n. 108) learned that the reservation Caddo formerly maintained a "band" of mescalbean doctors, perhaps comparable in organization to a medicine society. In addition, she implies that the Caddo at one time employed mescalbeans as "medicine" but adds that "this red bean is only worn nowadays for beads," A Caddo man wearing a bandoleer of what appear to be mescalbeans is pictured in a photograph taken by James Mooney in 1893 and reproduced by Swanton (1942:Plate 7, no. 2), but no museum specimens of mescalbeans associated with any of these Caddoan groups were encountered during the investigation.

Cheyenne

LaBarre (1969:106) quotes a Cheyenne informant (presumably a Southern Cheyenne from Oklahoma) to the effect that the Cheyenne employed mescalbeans therapeutically as an "eye-wash." There is no evidence that the Cheyenne, either Northern or Southern, ever consumed mescalbeans or maintained a mescalbean medicine society, but they have employed mescalbeans widely as items of material culture. In addition to the specimens described below, I have examined photographs in the National Anthropological Archives, Smithsonian Institution, depicting Southern Cheyenne men wearing (1) buckskin shirts with mescalbeans attached to the shoulder fringes (negative numbers 230, 294, and 296), (2) mescalbean bandoleers (negative numbers

217-A-1, 217-B-1 and 3, and 237) and (3) a hair ornament composed of two twisted leather (?) strands bearing what appears to be a mescalbean (negative number 23-C).

Specimen 15: <u>Man's tanned and fringed buckskin leggings</u>, 70 cm long at their longest point, 41 cm wide at the top and bottom. The major portion of the leggings are yellow in color with seven brown lines extending three quarters of the length of each legging from the bottom. A series of twisted leather strings are looped through the leggings to taper them. The leggings are painted a reddish brown color to the exterior of these strings and the edge of each legging is fringed for its entire length. This fringe is natural in color with blue lines painted on some of the individual fringes. The bottom of the leggings to the interior of the tapering strings are cut into short square fringes. Mescalbeans and metal springs are attached at intervals to the strings which taper the leggings, beginning at about one third of the length of the leggings from the top. There are twelve mescalbeans and two metal springs on the right legging (in a pattern of five mescalbeans, two springs and seven mescalbeans) and nine mescalbeans and one metal spring on the left legging (in a pattern of three mescalbeans, one metal spring, and six mescalbeans). The majority of mescalbeans are deep maroon in color though some are lighter than others. They appear to have been perforated with a hot drill. The mescalbeans are relatively small in size, ranging from 0.9 to 1.2 cm in length and 0.7 to 1.0 cm in width.

Smithsonian Institution, catalogue number CL 339. No collection or accession information available.

Specimen 16: <u>Hair ornament</u>. A rawhide strip, split into two strands for attachment to the wearer's hair, is tied to a bunch of unidentified fur. Four rawhide cords, consisting of two twisted rawhide strands each, connect the fur to four black (crow?) feathers. The ends of each of the four rawhide cords are wrapped around the base of one of the four feathers, all of which are notched at the top and trimmed along the edges. A perforated mescalbean is strung on each of the rawhide cords and located at the base of each of the four feathers. The four mescalbeans are relatively small in size, all being approximately 1.0 cm long and from 0.75 to 1.0 cm wide. They are of a uniform medium red color and apparently have been perforated with a cold drill.

Smithsonian Institution, catalogue number 165947, accession number 26674. Collected by H. R. Voth. No collection date or locality given. Acquired by purchase. Accession date: February 9, 1893.

Specimen 17: <u>Hair ornament</u>, 30 cm long (Fig. 9). Three small eagle feathers, cut at the top and along the edges, form the basic component of this ornament. The quill at the base of each of these feathers

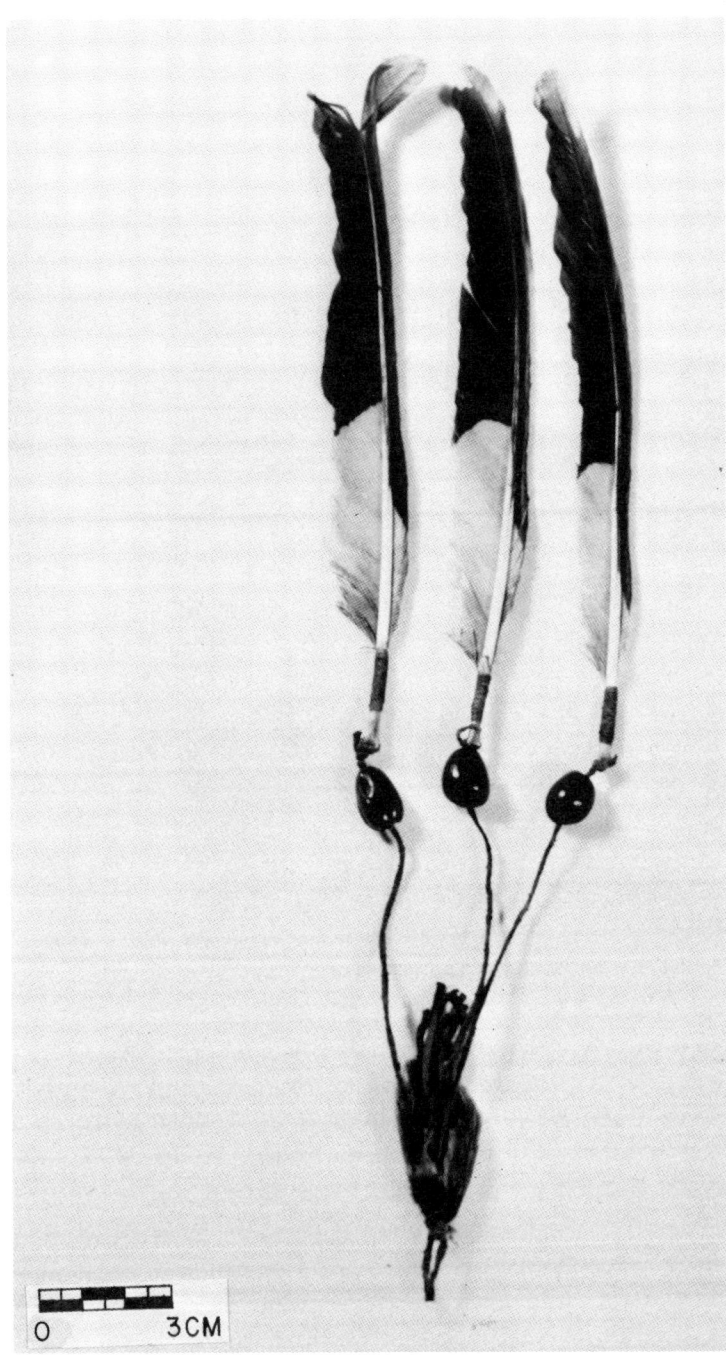

Figure 9. Specimen 17: A Cheyenne hair ornament composed of eagle feathers, mescalbeans, and a bunch of unidentified feathers connected by rawhide thongs. Smithsonian Institution, catalogue number 165946.

is split, turned back upon itself, and wrapped with sinew to form a loop. A dark brown rawhide string is tied to each of these loops, and a perforated mescalbean is strung on each of these strings. At the ends opposite the eagle feathers the strings are tied together and a bunch of small feathers, red with gray bases (a woodpecker topknot?), are attached. Two of the three mescalbeans are deep maroon in color, the third a lighter maroon. All the mescalbeans are approxminately 1.0 cm wide and range in length from 1.2 to 1.5 cm.

Smithsonian Institution, catalogue number 165946, accession number 26674. Collected by H. R. Voth. No collection date or locality given. Acquired by purchase. Accession date: February 9, 1893.

Specimen 18: This specimen is described as a "hair ornament. . . attached to scalp" in the catalogue information that accompanies it, but it could be a quirt. It consists of a lanyard made of brown and tan horsehair (?) plaited for 42.5 cm and elaborately spliced on each end. On one end, the fibers are loose beyond the splice, forming a sort of brush. On the opposite end, the two loose ends of a twisted rawhide string, tinted a reddish color, are attached to either side of the end of the splice. A white feather (possibly chicken) is attached to one end of these strings by sinew wrapped around its base. The feather has been cut at the top and along the edges and has three lines--two blue lines on the outside and a red line in the middle--painted across the feather about at midpoint and red paint smeared at its top. The rawhide string is looped and eight gold metal beads and three mescalbeans are strung on it. The arrangement is one mescalbean next to the end splice, followed by four gold metal beads, then another mescalbean, followed by four gold metal beads, a small piece of twisted wire (possibly copper), and finally another mescalbean. The extreme end of the loop, right next to the last mescalbean, is attached to a metal ring. A twisted rawhide string is tied to this ring by means of a dove's head knot and the two loose ends of the string are knotted to form a loop. The total length of the specimen is 89 cm. All three of the mescalbeans are deep maroon in color and relatively small, being approximately 1.0 cm long and .75 to 1.0 cm wide. The seeds seem to have been perforated by a hot drill, since they are discolored around the perforations. Also, the ends of the seeds are cut off flat around the perforations, rendering the holes rather large.

Smithsonian Institution, catalogue number 165953, accession number 26674. Collected by H. R. Voth. No collection date or locality given. Acquired by purchase. Accession date: February 9, 1893.

Specimen 19: Male doll, approximately 44 cm tall, classified in the accompanying catalogue information under the heading of "Children's Toys." The doll is dressed in a deeply fringed and beaded buckskin shirt, leggings, and buckskin moccasins. Five rows of quillwork serve as a belt to which is attached a fringed and beaded circular shield. The doll's hair is made from a human scalp. Several mescalbeans are attached to each of the shoulders and along each of the sides of the doll. Information on this specimen was secured through correspondence, so the size and color of these mescalbeans were not recorded.

Museum of the Plains Indian, catalogue number 1179, accession number 147. No collection date or locality given. Donated by the L. W. Hill Memorial Collection (G. N. R. R. Co.). Accession date: March 1, 1953.

Specimen 20: <u>Northern Cheyenne man's leggings</u>. Red beans, apparently perforated with a hot drill, are strung on strings down the sides of the leggings. Though these beans have not been positively identified, it is likely that they are the seeds of either or both <u>Sophora</u> <u>secundiflora</u> and <u>Erythrina</u> <u>flabelliformis</u>.

This specimen was collected in Montana by M. G. Chandler, who described it to Volney H. Jones in September, 1935. A more detailed description of it is not available at present.

Specimen 21: <u>Northern Cheyenne woman's beaded deerskin dress</u>, neatly tanned and very well made. The dress is composed of three pieces: the top consists of two pieces (the front and the back) attached to a one-piece bottom just below bust level. The sleeves and central portion of the bodice are cut from a single piece of material. The various pieces of the dress are sewn together with cotton thread on a sewing machine. Long fringes are attached to the sleeves of the dress, medium-length fringes to the bottom of the dress, and short fringes to both sides of the dress. The length of the dress from the shoulder to the bottom (including fringe) is 111 cm; the fringe is 10 cm long. The dress is 37 cm wide at the point where the top and bottom portions join; the sleeves are 24.5 cm long (including fringe). Two rows of metal bells are attached to the sides of the dress at the bottom. The dress is beaded in rows on the shoulder area across the middle of the bodice, on both the front and back sides, across the middle of the bottom part of the dress, and in a zigzag pattern along the hem at the bottom of the dress. The trade beads--which are red, white, blue, yellow, green, and orange and made from glass, "china," and metal--are arranged into geometrical designs. Tanned leather strings are looped through the dress, leaving loose ends, below the beaded row on the middle of the bodice (front and back), below the beaded row across the middle of the bottom portion of the dress, and at the top of the zigzags along the hem of the dress. A mescalbean is strung on each end of the loose ends of these strings. Below each mescalbean is a silver metal bead and below the metal bead the string is knotted. Twelve pairs of mescalbeans are present on the top portion of the dress, twelve pairs are attached to the middle of the bottom portion, and twenty pairs appear along the hem. Thus, there is a total of eighty-eight mescalbeans on the dress: forty-four on the front, forty-four on the back. The mescalbeans generally are of a uniform light maroon color and have been carefully perforated with a hot drill. They vary slightly in size, ranging from 1.1 to 1.7 cm in length and 0.9 to 1.1 cm in width.

Peabody Museum of Archaeology and Ethnology, Harvard University, catalogue number 10/24700, accession number 44-1. Collected by Mrs. Bradford H. Burnham, circa 1914, apparently in southern Montana. Donated by Dr. Thomas Barbour. Accession date: January 4, 1944. There is some confusion concerning the tribal affiliation of this dress. The original catalogue information classifies it as Crow, but subsequently it has been identified as Cheyenne and is exhibited as such.

Specimen 22: <u>Northern Cheyenne envelope-shaped rawhide bag</u>, (Fig. 10), 26.5 cm wide, 16 cm long. This bag consists of one piece of rawhide folded in half with a triangular-shaped flap on top. Two holes have been perforated in the center of the flap through which pass the two ends of a rawhide string looped through the center of the upper portion of the bag. The sides of the bag are sewn shut by a series of rawhide strings which are looped through several pairs of holes punched in the bag. These strings are knotted on the front of the bag and each string has two loose ends which extend beyond the knot. There are six pairs of loose ends on each side of the bag. Two mescalbeans are attached to the first loose end (counting from the top of the bag) of each pair, making a total of twenty-four mescalbeans attached to the bag. The back side of the bag is undecorated. The front side is painted in a design consisting of two rows of red and blue triangles separated by a red line and enclosed within a red rectangle. The spaces between the triangles are stained brownish-yellow upon which are drawn green horseshoe-shaped designs. The mescalbeans vary in color from brownish-red to deep maroon. They vary in size from 1.0 to 1.6 cm in length and 1.0 to 1.1 cm in width.

American Museum of Natural History, catalogue number 50.2/5841, accession number 1952-68. Purchased in Lamedeer, Montana, in 1914. Collector not given. The American Museum of Natural History apparently secured this specimen in 1952 from Mr. Gifford M. Proctor. It seems to have been a part of the "American Indian Collection of A. Phimister Proctor, Sculptor."

Specimen 23: <u>Northern Cheyenne mescalbean bandoleer</u>. This specimen consists of two strings of mescalbeans strung on fishing line, tied together with a conspicuous knot, but with no attachments. There are approximately eighty-five mescalbeans on each string, all of which are medium to large in size. They range in color from yellow to maroon. According to the owner, the mescalbeans were received in trade from Oklahoma. The bandoleer was worn over the left shoulder and under the right arm in the Northern Cheyenne's Omaha Dance; it was in no way associated with the Peyote Religion.

This specimen was obtained in 1952 by Robert Anderson from Daniel Old Bull, a Northern Cheyenne of Montana, and subsequently placed in the collections of the Florida State University Museum. It was examined by Volney Jones in 1952 at the University of Michigan.

Specimen 24: <u>Northern Cheyenne mescalbean necklace or bandoleer</u> (Fig 11). This specimen consists of ninety-nine <u>Sophora</u> <u>secundiflora</u> seeds, perforated apparently with a hot drill and strung on a cord made from twisted vegetal fibers or sinew. At intervals, very short black cloth strips, pieces of cotton cord, or portions of the vegetal or sinew cord of the necklace base are tied between the mescalbeans. The mescalbeans vary somewhat in color, ranging from deep maroon to a lighter brownish-red. They vary considerably in shape and size from 0.9 to 1.6 cm long and from 0.8 to 1.4 cm wide. Some of the seeds are cracked and discolored, apparently as a result of the use of heat in their perforation. The principal attachment to this necklace is a composite deer's tail, which consists of several deer tails fastened to a stick of unidentified wood. The white portions of the tails are attached to the lower part of the stick with the black portions of the tails at the upper end of the stick, giving an impression of one very large deer tail. The composite tail is 32.5 cm long. The mescalbean necklace is attached to the deer tail approximately 10 cm from the bottom of the stick by means of a rawhide cord dyed red. A red feather also is attached to the stick on the same side as the necklace by this cord. On the opposite side of the stick, the cord secures a fossil-type rock around which have been wrapped several red rawhide strings and a bunch of buffalo wool. The length of this specimen, including the deer tail attachment, is 53.5 cm (doubled) and approximately 112.5 cm when stretched out into a single strand.

Peabody Museum of Natural History, Yale University, catalogue number 9063, accession number 3635. Collected by Dr. George Bird Grinnell from Spotted Hawk of Lame Deer, Montana, on June 26, 1903. Received by donation from Dr. Grinnell on February 13, 1925. According to the catalogue information accompanying it, this specimen was "formerly worn and owned by old Spotted Wolf."

Specimen 25: <u>Northern Cheyenne necklace or bandoleer</u>. This specimen consists of forty-four <u>Sophora</u> <u>secundiflora</u> seeds and sixty-five <u>Erythrina</u> <u>flabelliformis</u> seeds strung on a rawhide string with no attachments. The manufacturer of this specimen apparently recognized the distinction between the <u>S. secundiflora</u> and <u>E. flabelliformis</u> seeds, since these two kinds of seeds are strung on the rawhide string in alternating groups as follows: two <u>S. secundiflora</u> seeds followed by fourteen <u>E. flabelliformis</u> seeds, then nine <u>S. secundiflora</u> seeds, seventeen <u>E. flabelliformis</u> seeds, etc. Both the <u>S. secundiflora</u> and <u>E. flabelliformis</u> seeds are maroon in color. Information on the size of the necklace, the range of sizes of the seeds, and the method of seed perforation was not secured since the specimen was on exhibit at the time of the investigation.

Peabody Museum of Natural History, Yale University, catalogue number 9062, accession number 3635. This specimen was collected by Dr. George Bird Grinnell in Lame Deer, Montana, on July 25, 1901, and was donated to the Peabody Museum by Dr. Grinnell on February 13, 1925. The catalogue information accompanying this specimen reads as follows: "String of red (seed) beads. Ma hē yŭnĭ ha wŭkkst. White Bird. Lame Deer, Mont. July 25, 1901. Sent by his brother, Two Crows, from the south more than 10 years ago."

Specimen 26: <u>Northern Cheyenne necklace</u> composed of ninety-six <u>Erythrina flabelliformis</u> seeds.

Field Museum of Natural History, catalogue number 14071/4011. This specimen was traded by the Field Museum to M. G. Chandler, who reports that it was collected from Northern Cheyenne of Lame Deer, Montana. It was examined in 1935 by Volney H. Jones. A more detailed description of it is not available.

Specimen 27: <u>Northern Cheyenne woman's "sack of medicine"</u> (Fig. 12). This medicine bag is made of a single piece of buffalo hide (the fur has not been removed) folded in half, the sides sewn together, and a little excess left to form a flap. Without the flap, the bag measures 28.5 cm wide and 16.5 cm long. The flap is 19 cm wide and 5.5 cm long. The flap and the side seams are decorated in geometric designs with glass trade beads colored yellow, dark blue, light blue, red, green, and white. Two silver metal tinklers containing yellowish-brown dyed horsehair are attached to each of the four corners of the bag, and one similar tinkler is attached to one corner of the flap. A rawhide thong, split in half, is tied to the flap and wrapped around the bundle to keep it shut. The bundle contains the following items: (1) Four <u>Sophora secundiflora</u> seeds, loose in the bag. The seeds have been perforated with a very small hot drill (perhaps a needle) and the largest of the seeds is cracked, apparently resulting from the manner of perforation. Three of the seeds are deep maroon in color while the fourth is a lighter brownish-red. The seeds are relatively small, ranging from 1.0 to 1.4 cm long and from 0.6 to 1.1 cm wide. (2) Five pieces of an unidentified white, fibrous plant material resembling a rootstock. (3) Four pieces of another kind of plant material, also unidentified and resembling a rootstock. (4) One unidentified disk-shaped fungus 7 cm in diameter. (5) One stalactite (?) 2.9 cm long. (6) One unidentified shell, 4.6 cm long. (7) One unidentified oval-shaped translucent rock, 3 1/2 cm by 2 3/4 cm. (8) Five small leather medicine bags, four containing unidentified vegetal materials (one of which has a piece of dentalium strung on its rawhide tiestring) and the fifth an unidentified piece of bone.

Peabody Museum of Natural History, Yale University, catalogue number 9087, accession number 3635. Collected by Dr. George Bird Grinnell from Mrs. White Bird of Lame Deer, Montana, on June 25, 1903. Received by donation from Dr. Grinnell on February 13, 1925.

Figure 10. Specimen 22: A Northern Cheyenne rawhide bag with mescalbeans along both sides. American Museum of Natural History, catalogue number 50.2/5841.

Figure 11. Specimen 24: A Northern Cheyenne mescalbean necklace, or bandoleer, with a composite deertail attachment. Peabody Museum of Natural History, Yale University, catalogue number 9063.

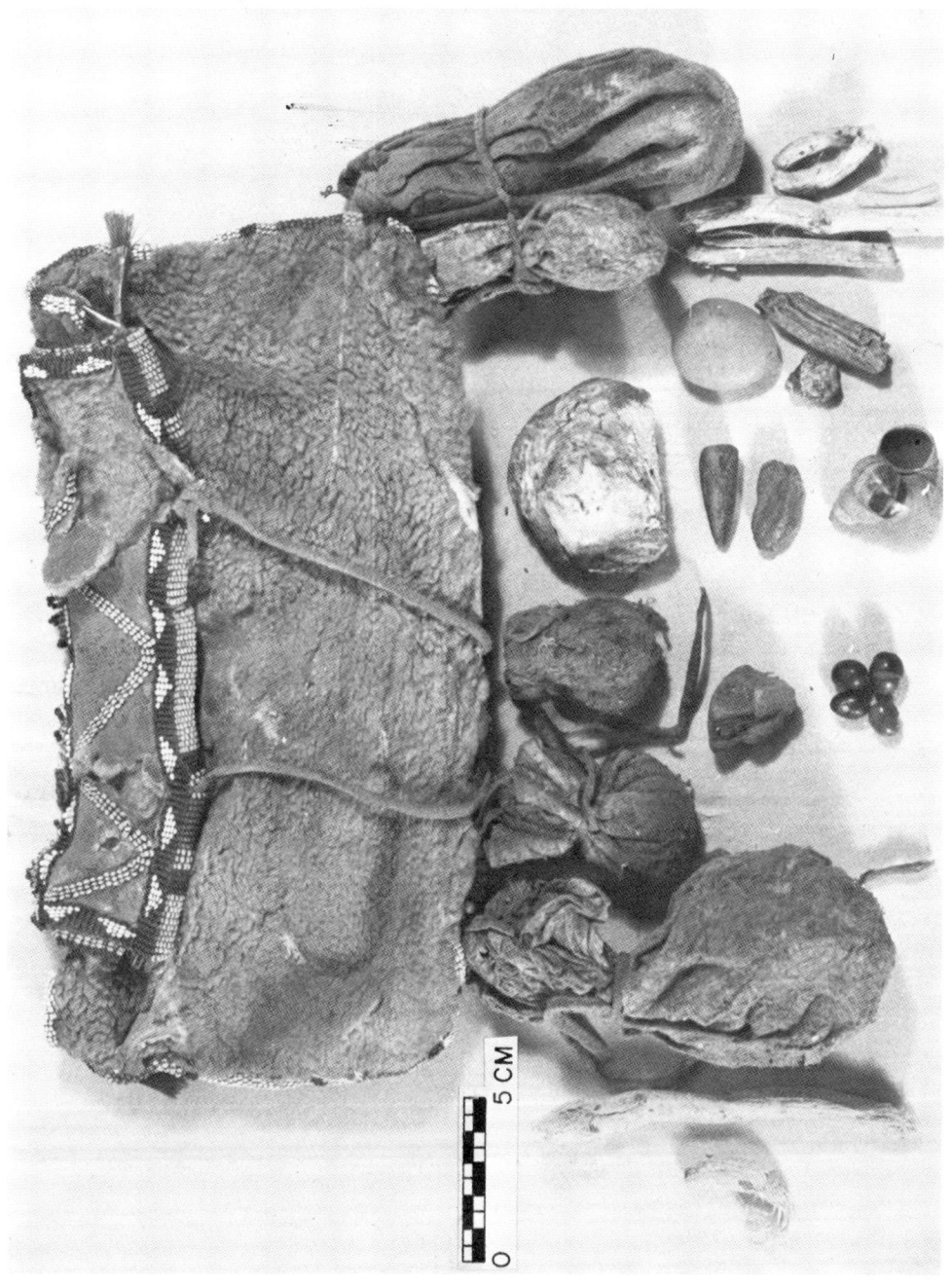

Figure 12. Specimen 27: A Northern Cheyenne woman's "sack of medicine." Four mescalbeans appear in the bottom row, center. Peabody Museum of Natural History, Yale University, catalogue number 9087.

Specimen 28: <u>Southern Cheyenne (?) hair ornament</u>, approximately 16.25 cm long. This specimen consists of a bunch of unidentified small feathers, some brown and yellow, others black and white. All the feathers are cut in various ways at their tops and along their sides. The base of each feather is wrapped with sinew under which are attached very small red feathers and a rawhide string dyed green. The rawhide strings are then knotted to form a bunch. At the base of the bunch of feathers and strings is another leather string to which is attached one mescalbean followed by three silver metal beads with a knot tied at the bottom of the string. The two loose ends of the string below the knot are themselves knotted to form a loop for attachment to the hair. The mescalbean, which has been perforated with a hot drill, is maroon and rather small (0.8 cm long and 1.0 cm wide).

Smithsonian Institution, catalogue number 392557, accession number 198353. Collector unknown. Collection locality: if the identification of this specimen as Southern Cheyenne is correct, then it probably was collected in Oklahoma. Acquired through anonymous deposit. Accession date: May 21, 1953.

Coahuilteco

At the time of European contact, bands of Coahuilteco-speakers inhabited portions of southern Texas and adjacent northern Mexico where <u>Sophora</u> <u>secundiflora</u> occurs in abundance. Yet information regarding their use of mescalbeans is restricted to the following question, posed in an eighteenth century Spanish confessional (García 1760:15): "Have you eaten <u>frixolillo</u>? / Did it intoxicate you?" The question regarding <u>frixolillo</u>, a Spanish vernacular term for mescalbeans, immediately follows a similar inquiry regarding the consumption of peyote. Troike (1962:954) suggests that the Coahuiltecans may have consumed mescalbeans and peyote on an interchangeable basis in communal ceremonies. There is no published evidence that any of the Coahuiltecan groups employed mescalbeans as items of material culture, and no museum specimens of Coahuiltecan provenience were encountered during the investigation.

Comanche

Berlandier (1969:95) implies that the Comanche consumed an emetic and purgative decoction of mescalbeans in the context of their first fruits ceremonies. Opler's (1940:190n. 2) Lipan Apache informants had heard that the Comanche mixed mescalbeans and peyote, but they do not indicate for what purposes or in what contexts this mixture was employed. Clark (1885:141), who visited the Comanche in 1881 on their reservation in Indian Territory, reports that Comanche Deer Dancers pretended to swallow and then extract "red beans" from their chests during the performance of their ceremonies. However, there is no evidence that any of the Comanche bands maintained a medicine society comparable in organization to the mescalbean medicine societies of the Prairie groups. More recently, Jones (1972:58) reports that a contemporary Comanche doctor cures earaches and sores deep in the ear with a decoction prepared from ground mescalbeans. Though the Comanche employed mescalbeans widely as items of material culture, surprisingly no Comanche buckskin shirts with mescalbeans attached to them were encountered in any of the museum collections examined during the investigation. However, the popularity of using mescalbeans in this fashion among Comanche men and boys is demonstrated in several photographs housed in the collections of the National Anthropological Archives, Smithsonian Institution (for example, negative numbers 1752-B, 1761-B, T-15393, 42931-C, and 42998-B).

Specimen 29: Man's tanned leggings. This specimen was on exhibit at the time of this investigation, so a complete description of it was not made. Only the left legging was visible. Strips of green, red, white, dark blue, and yellow trade beads are sewn along the fringed edges and bottom of the legging. A series of buckskin thongs, each with two loose ends are looped through the legging to taper them. These loose ends are twisted together to form cords to which are attached feathers and mescalbeans. There are nine mescalbeans attached to the leggings, one on each of the bottom nine strings. The leggings are dyed red between the tapering strings and the edge of the legging.

Museum of the American Indian (Heye Foundation), catalogue number 16/5532. No collection date or locality given. Presented by Mrs. William I. Lander from the collection of Captain W. I. Lander. Accession date: 1929.

Specimen 30: <u>Girl's dress</u>, 70 cm long from shoulder to bottom, 41 cm wide between the shoulders, 80 cm wide at the bottom; the sleeves are 35 cm long. This dress is composed of two pieces of tanned buckskin, dyed yellow and sewn together with cotton thread along the shoulders and the sides. The sleeves, made from separate pieces of buckskin, have been cuffed and are sewn on the dress at the shoulders. Two triangular-shaped pieces of buckskin are sewn to the neck, one on the front, the other on the back. Strips of long fringe are sewn onto the dress at the shoulders, on the back side of the sleeves, and on the triangular flaps at the neck. In addition, the bottom corners of the dress have been cut into fringes. Strips of beading--made of red, white, yellow, green, blue, black, and pink glass trade beads arranged in geometrical designs--are placed over the seams of the dress where the fringed strips are sewn onto the triangular flaps, along the top of the shoulders, and at the point where the sleeves join the shoulders. Bunches of small orange and yellow feathers wrapped with sinew at their bases and attached to buckskin strings are tied onto one of the fringes on each shoulder of the dress. A series of tanned buckskin strings are looped through the upper portion of the dress on both sides at about breast level. On what appears to be the front side, three mescalbeans are attached to three of these strings, one to each string. Three mescalbeans also are strung on three of the fringes at each of the shoulders on this same side of the dress. No mescalbeans appear on the opposite side of the dress. Instead a medicine packet--made of a blue cotton handkerchief with pink and white lace-like borders and tied shut with the blue and white border from another handkerchief--is attached to the two ends of one string that passes through the mid-back part of the dress. There are a total of nine mescalbeans present on this dress. They are uniformly of a medium red color with a faint tint of brown. They all are medium sized, 1.0 to 1.3 cm long and all but one 1.0 cm wide; the exception is 1.2 cm wide. All the seeds have been perforated with a hot drill but none are cracked or broken.

American Museum of Natural History, catalogue number 50.1/6329, accession number 1911-46. Collected by P. E. Goddard, apparently in Oklahoma sometime during 1911. Accession date: 1911.

Specimen 31: <u>Girl's fringed buckskin dress</u>, composed of separate bodice and bottom parts sewn together. The bodice portion is a yellowish tan color, the bottom portion a light tan. A strip of red felt bordered by a beaded band of white and blue trade beads lines the neck region of the dress, both front and back. A light red line is drawn across the middle of the bodice, front and back, below which are looped a series of rawhide strings, each with two loose ends. On the front side, two mescalbeans are attached to each of the ends of every other string with two exceptions. In the case of one string, one end is broken off, leaving space for only two mescalbeans; in another instance, one of the seeds is <u>Erythrina flabelliformis</u> rather than <u>Sophora secundiflora</u>. On the back side, only two strings have mescalbeans strung on them: the third string from either side has two mescalbeans attached to each of its ends. On the bottom section, front and back, just below the point where the bottom section joins the bodice, a second row of strings is looped through. Shells are attached to each end of every other string on the front while nothing is attached to these strings on the back side. Next, several rows of white and blue glass trade beads are sewn across the middle of the bottom portion of the dress, front and back, below which is looped another row of rawhide strings. There are no attachments to these strings on the front side; two white beads are attached to the ends of one of these strings on the back side. Another row of blue and white trade beads is arranged in a zigzag pattern just above the hem of the dress. Six pairs of metal tinklers are attached to the dress on each side by means of looped rawhide strings at the highest points of the zigzag pattern. The dress is painted red between the beaded row and the bottom fringe. A flap is sewn on either side of the bottom of the dress to which are attached alternating rows of blue and white trade beads and metal tinklers. The dress is 76.5 cm long from the neck to the bottom exluding the fringe (83 cm with fringe included) and 65 cm wide at the shoulders including the sleeves but excluding the fringe (96 cm wide with fringe included). It is 44 cm wide at the bottom and 29 cm wide at the point where the bodice and bottom portions join. A total of thirty-nine <u>Sophora secundiflora</u> seeds and one <u>Erythrina flabelliformis</u> seed are present on the dress; two additional seeds, whether <u>S</u>. <u>secundiflora</u> or <u>E</u>. <u>flabelliformis</u>, seem to have been lost. All the seeds are deep maroon in color and apparently have been polished, either intentionally or through use. All the seeds have been perforated with a hot drill and the ends of the <u>E</u>. <u>flabelliformis</u> seed have been cut off. The <u>E</u>. <u>flabelliformis</u> seed is larger and more bean-shaped than the majority of the <u>S</u>. <u>secundiflora</u> seeds. The <u>E</u>. <u>flabelliformis</u> seed is 1.5 cm long and 1.0 cm wide. The <u>S</u>. <u>secundiflora</u> seeds range in size from 1.1 to 1.5 cm in length and 0.8 to 1.3 cm in width.

University Museum, University of Pennsylvania, catalogue number 45-15-265. No collection date or locality given. Purchased from the Charles H. Stevens Collection under the aegis of Mrs. Owen Stevens. Accession date: 1947 (?).

Specimen 32: <u>Child's medicine beads</u>. This specimen, a simple mescalbean necklace, consists of one hundred and four perforated mescalbeans on a buckskin string. A disk of form material covered with buckskin is attached to the string between the thirty-first and thirty-second mescalbeans from the point where the ends of the string are tied together. The color of the mescalbeans varies from light to dark maroon, but all the seeds show signs of having been intentionally darkened and perhaps polished. Generally medium in size but with some variation, the seeds range from 1.0 to 1.7 cm in length and 0.8 to 1.3 cm in width. The entire specimen is 62 cm long when doubled and approximately 130 cm long when stretched out into a single strand. This length is comparable to that of mescalbean necklaces worn by adults and although it seems a bit long for a child, it could easily have been worn doubled. It is classified in the catalogue information that accompanies it as designed for use by a child and is exhibited with children's clothes.

Museum of the American Indian (Heye Foundation), catalogue number 2/1416. Collected by M. R. Harrington in Oklahoma, circa 1909. Accession date: 1909.

Specimen 33: <u>Mescalbean necklace with peyote bag</u>, 77 cm long (doubled), 159 cm long (as single strand). The necklace is composed of one hundred and twenty-five mescalbeans strung on a buckskin string. Two rattlesnake rattles are tied to the right side of the necklace with a buckskin thong which in turn serves to attach the necklace to the right side of a fringed buckskin pouch. On the left side of the pouch, a buckskin thong beaded with light blue trade beads is wrapped around a small bunch of unidentified purple and orange feathers and a braided strand of human hair. A buckskin thong attaches this pendant to the necklace and the necklace to the left side of the pouch. The two ends of the necklace extend along the sides of the pouch and are knotted at the end. The fringe on the bottom of the pouch is decorated with trade beads of various sizes and colors. In addition, a small silver bird is strung on one of the fringes. The bird more closely resembles a songbird such as a swallow than an eagle or thunderbird. The pouch and its flap are decorated along their edges with dark blue, light blue, and white glass trade beads. The principal portion of both the pouch and flap bear a spiral design in clear glass beads around a metal brad. The bag is empty but presumably contained at one time a peyote button. The mescalbeans are maroon in color with some slight variation from dark to light. They have been perforated with a hot drill. They vary in size from 1.0 to 1.7 cm in length and 0.6 to 1.3 cm in width.

Museum of the American Indian (Heye Foundation), catalogue number 2/1534. Collected by M. R. Harrington in Oklahoma, circa 1909. Accession date: 1909.

Specimen 34: <u>Mescalbean and trade bead necklace</u> with bear claw attached. Identified as a "bear claw war charm" in the catalogue information accompanying it, this specimen is 18 cm long (doubled and excluding the bear claw) and the bear claw is 10 cm long. When stretched out into a single strand, the necklace measures 40 cm. The necklace consists chiefly of blue and green china beads (with one black bead) strung on a buckskin thong with a mescalbean placed after every six to eight china beads. At the midpoint of the necklace is attached a perforated bear claw decorated at its base with small blue, yellow, white, and red glass trade beads. The loose ends of the string are unadorned and apparently were tied around the wearer's neck each time the necklace was worn (since the beaded portion of the necklace provides a circumference too small to be slipped over an adult's head). There is a total of six mescalbeans on this necklace. They are deep maroon in color and apparently were perforated with a hot drill, though there is little evidence of heat discoloration. They all are of medium size, but no exact measurements of them were made.

Museum of the American Indian (Heye Foundation), catalogue number 2/1711. Collected in Oklahoma by M. R. Harrington, circa 1909. Accession date: 1909.

Specimen 35: <u>Mescalbean necklace</u> and bear claw, 43 cm long when doubled and approximately 90 cm long when stretched out as a single strand. This rather short necklace, identified as a "bear claw charm" in the accompanying catalogue information, consists of thirty mescalbeans and three shells strung on a buckskin thong. An undecorated bear claw is perforated and strung on the necklace at its midpoint. On the wearer's left is attached a cluster of feathers (possibly from a flicker). A rawhide string and small pieces of red feathers are attached to the base of each feather by sinew wrapping. The rawhide strings are then tied together and the entire bunch of feathers is tied onto the necklace. The arrangement of seeds, shells, and attachments on the necklace is as follows (from the bear claw around to the right): six mescalbeans, one shell, five mescalbeans, the cluster of feathers, one shell, two mescalbeans, the knotted and loose ends of the thong, seven mescalbeans, one shell, ten mescalbeans, and, finally, the bear claw. All the mescalbeans are very dark, ranging from almost black to a deep maroon. They have been perforated with a hot drill and many of the seeds are cracked and wrinkled; one is broken in half. In addition, the ends of many of the mescalbeans have been cut off flat to enlarge the circumference of their perforations. This gives the impression that they are almost square in shape, but many of the mescalbeans are square-shaped naturally and none are particularly bean-shaped. They vary somewhat in size, ranging from 0.8 to 1.2 cm in length and 1.0 to 1.2 cm in width.

Museum of the American Indian (Heye Foundation), catalogue number 2/1707. Collected by M. R. Harrington in Oklahoma, probably in 1909. Accession date: 1909.

Specimen 36: <u>Comanche and Wichita mescalbean necklace</u>, 52 cm long. This specimen consists of forty mescalbeans strung onto a fiber cord composed of several strands of unidentified twisted fiber. The necklace is in very poor condition having been broken into five segments. The mescalbeans are generally dark maroon, although there is some slight variation in shade from seed to seed. They have been perforated by burning. They vary in size from 1.0 to 1.7 cm long and 0.9 to 1.2 cm wide. There also is some variation in shape.

Smithsonian Institution, catalogue number 6942, accession number 1317 (?). Collected by Dr. Edward Palmer, probably in Indian Territory in 1868. Accession date: November 11, 1868(?).

Crow

There is no published information indicating that the Crow ever employed mescalbeans for any purpose. Two mescalbean specimens that perhaps are of Crow provenience were encountered during this investigation: (1) a lance (specimen 14) also attributed possibly to the Arapaho; and (2) a dress (specimen 21) originally identified as Crow but subsequently designated as Northern Cheyenne. None of the Crow photographs on file in the National Anthropological Archives, Smithsonian Institution, depict individuals wearing seeds that could with any certainty be identified as mescalbeans.

Delaware

Voegelin (n.d.) learned in 1939 that Delaware individuals of the Caney River group located near Dewey, Oklahoma, employed mescalbeans only as ornaments. There is no indication that any of the Delaware groups ever used mescalbeans for anything other than seed beads. No Delaware specimens of mescalbeans were discovered in the museum collections examined during the investigation.

Hidatsa

According to Howard (n.d.), Hidatsa peyotists wear mescalbean bandoleers as components of their Peyote Religion paraphernalia. No other information regarding the Hidatsa use of mescalbeans has been located and no mescalbean specimens attributable to the Hidatsa were encountered during the investigation.

Iowa

The members of the Iowa Red Medicine Dancing Society consumed a decoction of baked and crushed mescalbeans. Emesis and purging seem to have been the primary effects desired, but stimulation and the phenomenon of seeing red also are reported (Hamilton in Dorsey 1894:429; Skinner 1915:718-19; Harrington in Skinner 1926:245-47). Iowa warriors donned amulets from the Red Medicine War Bundle for protection during battles and the bundle itself was thought to bring success in hunting (particularly buffalo hunting), horse racing, horse raiding, and military encounters in general (Skinner 1915:718-19; Harrington in Skinner 1926:247).

Specimen 37: Man's leggings, approximately 72.5 cm long, described and pictured in Skinner (1926:261, 332-33, Plate XLV, Figures 2 and 3). According to Skinner

> The leggings are made of very soft tanned deerskin and have a narrow ankle cuff which is slightly fringed. The garment is made out of a single piece of skin, cut according to the pattern shown, and sewed or rather caught together with thongs along the outline of the leg. The thongs do not pass all the way through the outer piece of deerskin, but are pushed through only a part of it, so that they are not visible from the front, when the leggings are worn. On the rear the thongs are brought through and knotted closed to where they emerge. The five or six inches remaining at each end serve as ornaments. To one of these thongs, in each case, is attached a perforated scarlet mescal bean, the maka shutze, or 'red medicine,' of the Ioway.

> When the legging was sewed up to fit the limb, in
> the manner described, the residual leather formed two
> flaps. These flaps were not allowed to remain as they
> were, as is the case among the Central Algonkian, but
> were neatly stitched together with thongs about half
> an inch from the border, so that they now form only a
> single heavy flap. In addition, separate thongs,
> ranging from nine inches in length at the bottom to
> four and one-half at the thigh, were attached in-
> dividually along the border, further binding the two
> edges together, and forming a handsome fringe. On the
> outside, or front of the garment the space between the
> seams made in the manner described, is filled with a
> narrow stripe of white beadwork bearing a delicate
> geometric design in several colors, and a close set
> row of brass headed tacks.

Skinner suggests that the leggings "may be of the modified Kiowa-Comanche type generally affected by members of the Peyote cult among all Oklahoma tribes," but notes that similar pairs are employed by Iowas who are not members of the Peyote church and photos show Iowas wearing similar leggings "forty and fifty years ago," circa 1876 to 1886.

Milwaukee Public Museum, catalogue number 30558 a-b. Collected from Robert Small, "Walks-from-the-Creation-on," an Iowa of Oklahoma, by Alanson Skinner.

Specimen 38: *A mescalbean necklace*, composed of about one hundred and fifty mescalbeans perforated and strung on red commercial twine. According to Skinner (1926:263), "It has a shell gorget of small size, with scalloped edges and incised border decoration, as a pendant." This specimen was examined in 1933 by Volney H. Jones who determined that the seed beads making up the necklace are *Sophora secundiflora*.

Milwaukee Public Museum, catalogue number 30555/7322. Collected by Alanson Skinner from Mr. Charles Tohee, an Iowa of Oklahoma. No collection date given.

Specimen 39: *Mescalbean necklace or bandoleer*, 72 cm long (doubled) approximately 150 cm long (stretched out as a single strand). This specimen consists of one hundred and seventeen mescalbeans strung on a single strand of commercial cotton cord. A strip of unidentified fur is wrapped around the necklace and two metal rings are strung on it. The mescalbeans are uniformly deep maroon with only the slightest variation from seed to seed. They apparently have been perforated with a hot drill but there is little evidence of heat discoloration. They vary somewhat in size, ranging from 0.9 to 1.4 cm long and 0.8 to 1.4 cm wide.

Museum of the American Indian (Heye Foundation), catalogue number 2/6833. Collected by M. R. Harrington in Oklahoma; no collection date given. Accession date: between 1910 and 1913.

Specimen 40: <u>Red Bean Medicine Bundle</u>, referred to in the accompanying catalogue information as <u>mankanteutzi</u>, 'red bean medicine' (Fig. 13). This bundle consists of three major components, which will be described below. These components were not contained within a single bundle wrapper but were stored together in a cardboard box and associated in the accompanying catalogue information. The three major components are: (1) a rawhide wrapper containing: One three-seeded <u>Sophora secundiflora</u> pod with a red cord wrapped around one of the depressions between the seeds. Two perforations are made on either side of one end of the pod. A perforated rawhide packet wrapped tightly around what appears to be mescalbeans (the seed scars are not visible). A rawhide thong is knotted in the middle around the end of this packet with its two ends hanging loose. Another perforated rawhide packet containing again what seem to be two mescalbeans (hilum not visible). A red ribbon is tied to this packet. Several twists of an unidentified plant material. Two loose mescalbeans, one a dull medium red color, the other a shiny deep maroon color. Four small seeds, apparently <u>Abrus precatorius</u> L. (also a member of the Leguminosae). These seeds are maroon with a black spot around their seed scars. One of these seeds is almost black, apparently the result of special treatment. (2) A small rawhide bag (12 cm by 4 cm) containing sixteen mescalbeans, none of which have been perforated. These mescalbeans vary considerably in color, ranging from black through deep maroon to medium red. They range in size from 1.1 cm to 1.6 cm in length and from 1.0 to 1.2 cm in width, and vary in shape from bean-shaped to almost square. (3) A striped trade cloth wrapper with floral designs containing: A bunch of buffalo wool. One three-seeded <u>Sophora secundiflora</u> pod with two holes punched in one end of the pod, one on either side. A rawhide string is wrapped around one of the depressions between the seeds and serves to attach the pod to the middle of a group of three ribbons (one light purple, one red, and one blue). A strip of cloth with leaf designs in brown, white, and green is wrapped up in these ribbons.

American Museum of Natural History. The three components are catalogued as 50.1/8056 a, b, and c respectively, accession number 1914-45. Collected in 1914 by Alanson Skinner in Perkins, Oklahoma. Accession date: August 31, 1914.

Specimen 41: <u>Red Bean War Bundle.</u> A woven rush bag serves as the container of this bundle, which includes the following items: (1) two calico wrappers containing four medicine packages; (2) a woven bag containing a cloth pouch, inside of which is a package containing a moleskin and a snake fang wrapped in paper; (3) a calico wrapper containing a snake skin; (4) a leather bag containing a pouch in which are a stone and three medicine packages; (5) a cloth bag containing a package that

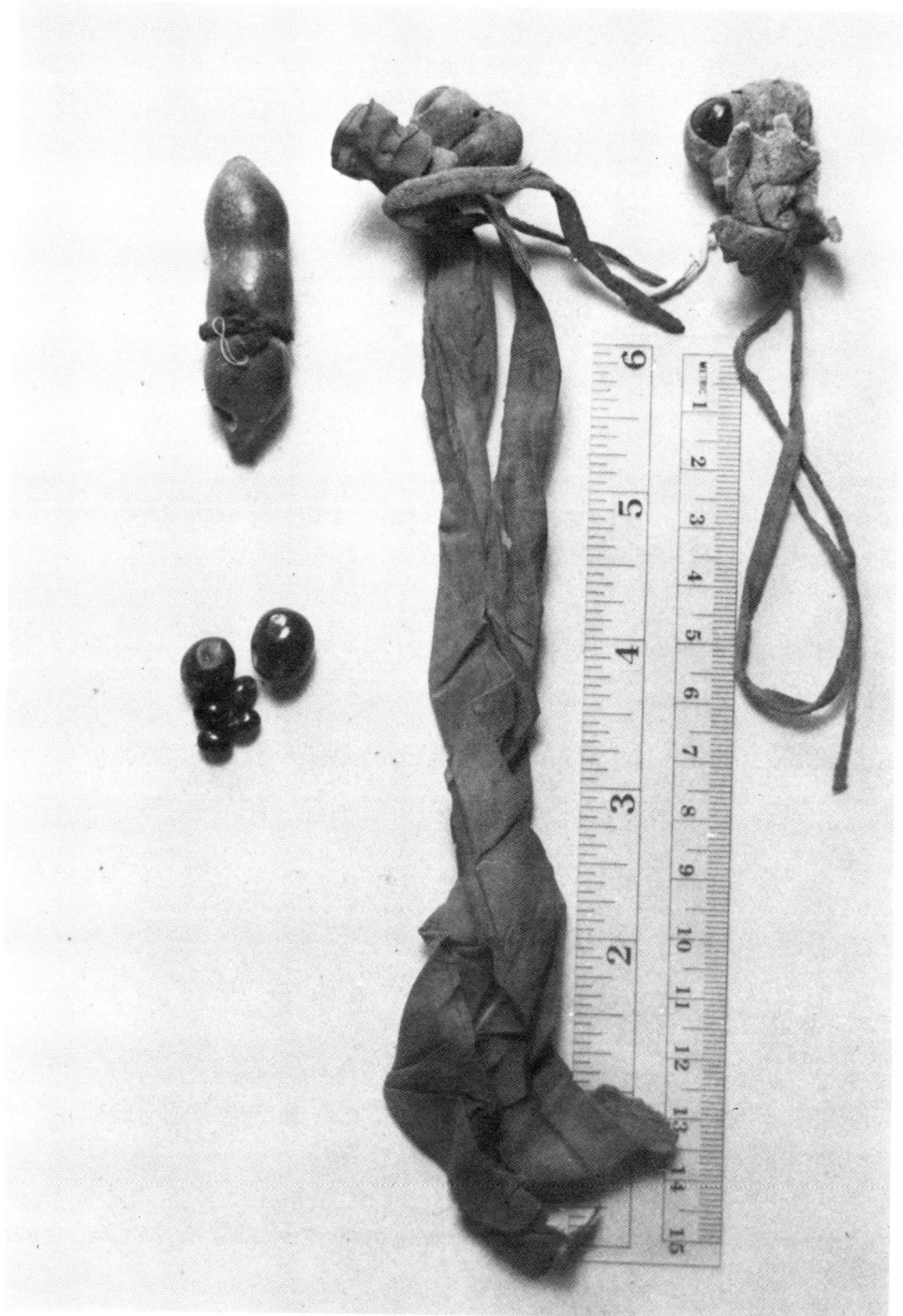

Figure 13. Specimen 40: The partial contents of an Iowa Red Bean medicine bundle. Depicted here are perforated packets of mescalbeans, a perforated Sophora secundiflora pod, two mescalbeans, and four seeds of Abrus precatorius. American Museum of Natural History, catalogue number 50.1/8056c.

holds two bullets and several roots; (6) three cane whistles; and (7) a calico wrapper containing two pieces of animal skin in which are a medicine package and two bunches of feathers, to one of which a buckskin bag containing a mescalbean pod is attached. Skinner (1926:Plate XL, Figures 5, 6, and 7; cf. pp. 245-47) pictures three components of this bundle: a bunch of feathers to the base of which is attached a perforated rawhide packet tightly enclosing what appear to be two mescalbeans; a bunch of buffalo wool, with a similar rawhide packet containing again what seem to be two mescalbeans, and a cane whistle, smeared with white paint. I did not personally examine this specimen.

Museum of the American Indian (Heye Foundation), catalogue number 2/8733. Collected by M. R. Harrington in Oklahoma probably in 1910. Accession date: between 1910 and 1913.

Kansa

Dorsey (1884:351n. 21; 1894:416, 418, 419) reports that the Kansa possessed "Red Medicine" and suggests that they employed it as a fetish. A Kansa shaman also informed him that "the red medicine" was one of eight classes of objects employed by shamans in shooting performances, and another individual (apparently a Kansa) told him that his father had owned "a red medicine, which was used for women who desired to become enciente, for horses, and for causing good dreams." It is impossible to determine if the Kansa term glossed as "Red Medicine" referred to mescalbeans at all or, if so, exclusively to mescalbeans. It is likely that it did refer in part to mescalbeans since Dorsey describes this "Red Medicine" as if it was identical to the Red Medicine of other neighboring Siouan-speaking groups, which can be identified with some certainty as mescalbeans. Dorsey does not indicate if the Kansa maintained a mescalbean medicine society or if they ever consumed mescalbeans. No additional published information exists regarding the Kansa use of mescalbeans, and no museum specimens of mescalbeans attributed to the

Kansa were discovered during the investigation. However, a photograph of a Kansa man wearing a bandoleer of what appear to be mescalbeans was examined in the National Anthropological Archives, Smithsonian Institution (negative number 52862) and is reproduced in Powers (1972:35).

Kickapoo

Schultes (1937:145) reports that the Kickapoo employ ground-up mescalbeans boiled in water and strained through a cloth to cure earaches, presumably by pouring the decoction directly into the affected ear canal. Other than this therapeutic use, the Kickapoos are not reported to have used mescalbeans for anything other than seed beads. In addition to the mescalbean necklace described below, I have examined a series of studio photographs housed in the National Anthropological Archives, Smithsonian Institution, which depict a Kickapoo man wearing a buckskin shirt with mescalbeans attached to the shoulder fringe (negative numbers 727-D-1, 2, 3, and 4).

Specimen 42: Mescalbean necklace worn during peyote ceremonies. This specimen was on exhibit at the time of investigation and a complete description of it was not made. All identifiable seeds are Sophora secundiflora and all are generally of a deep maroon color.
Museum of the American Indian (Heye Foundation), catalogue number 2/4906. Collected by M. R. Harrington in Oklahoma, circa 1909. Accession date: 1909.

Kiowa

There is no evidence that the Kiowa ever consumed mescalbeans on a regular basis or that they maintained a society in any way comparable to a mescalbean medicine society. However, a Kiowa man is said to have

Figure 14. Two Kiowa individuals wearing mescalbeans. The woman has mescalbeans strung on buckskin thongs across the front of her dress. The man wears a mescalbean bandoleer and has at least one and possibly two mescalbeans attached to the edge of his left legging. Photograph taken in 1913 by DeLancey Gill in Washington, D.C. Reproduced courtesy of the National Anthropological Archives, Smithsonian Institution (negative number 1475-C).

consumed a single mescalbean prior to breaking a wild horse (La Barre 1969:106), and Howard (1962:125) suggests, on the basis of information recently secured, that the Kiowa may have at one time used mescalbeans in "shooting" rites. The Kiowas have employed mescalbeans primarily as attachments to a wide range of items of material cuture and as seed beads in the manufacture of necklaces and bandoleers. La Barre (1969: 26) reports that the Kiowa formerly wore mescalbean bandoleers in battle. In more recent times, mescalbean bandoleers have become prominent items of Kiowa peyote ceremonial paraphernalia. The Kiowa also attach mescalbeans to other peyote-associated items. La Barre (1969:106) relates that one Kiowa peyote leader attached mescalbeans to his moccasin heel-fringe as a protection against menstrual blood pollution and that another peyote member strung a mescalbean on the thong of his gourd rattle. However, modern Kiowa use of mescalbeans is not restricted to peyote contexts, nor have mescalbeans been employed exclusively by men (Fig. 14). Momaday (1974:13) describes the regalia of modern Kiowa gourd dancers as including mescalbean bandoleers, and photographs in the National Anthropological Archives, Smithsonian Institution, document the Kiowa practice of attaching mescalbeans to women's dresses (negative numbers 1475-A, B, and C; 1476-A,1, 2, and 3).

Specimen 43: <u>Man's tanned and fringed buckskin leggings</u>, 89 cm long at the longest point, 41 cm wide at the top (including fringe), and 45 cm wide at the bottom (including fringe). The leggings are tinted green and the fringe, which extends the entire length of the leggings, is dyed dark green. A strip of trade beads composed of blue zigzags on a white background extends along the sides and bottom of both sides of both leggings. The seams of the leggings down the sides are stitched with thread. Tan and green leather strips are attached to one side of the leggings next to the seam. Lengths of horsehair bound at the base with blue and white porcupine quills are attached to the tan strips while mescalbeans and copper colored metal beads are strung on the green strips. A series of circular designs done in red and green--with two or three feather designs made from red, white, and blue glass trade beads located at the bottom of each circle--extend the length of the leggings between the seam and the fringe. On the opposite side of the leggings, only green leather strings are attached to the seam and these are fewer in number than the strings on the oppostie side. Mescalbeans and copper colored metal beads are attached to these green leather strips. On this side, the circular design is replaced by a crucifix design done in red and white trade beads. A total of forty-five mescalbeans, twenty-three copper colored beads, and eighteen horsehair strips are present on this specimen. The mescalbeans vary in color from deep to light maroon and have been perforated with a hot drill. They all are of a rather uniform medium size, ranging from 1.2 to 1.5 cm in length and 0.8 to 1.2 cm in width.

Smithsonian Institution, catalogue number 357902, accession number 113605. Collected in Oklahoma; no date given. Acquired by bequest from the Estate of Victor J. Evans. Accession date: March 26, 1931.

Specimen 44: <u>Man's leggings</u>, worn during Peyote Religion activities. A single mescalbean is attached to each of eight strings looped through each legging along its outer edge. A total of sixteen mescalbeans are present on this specimen. I have not examined this specimen personally but have had access to a description of it made by Volney H. Jones when he examined it in 1933.

Field Museum of Natural History, catalogue number 67811, numbers 1 and 2. Collected in 1902 by George A. Dorsey, presumably in Oklahoma.

Specimen 45: <u>Man's fringed buckskin shirt</u>, 43 cm wide between the shoulders and 68.5 cm long from the shoulders to the bottom of the shirt; the sleeves are 43 cm long. The shirt consists of six separate pieces of leather sewn together: the front, the back, the two sleeves, and two triangular-shaped, heavily fringed pieces sewn on at the neck, front and back. The sleeves are cuffed and have a single row of white trade beads sewn on to the edge of each cuff. In addition, a row of buckskin strings are looped through the shirt across the chest on the front and the middle of the back. Strips of long fringes also are attached to the shoulders and sleeves of the shirt. Six mescalbeans are strung on the fringe of each of the shoulders and another mescalbean is attached to the fringe of the front triangular piece. The fringe on the sleeves and at the shoulders is very stiff, apparently having been rubbed with clay. The mescalbeans attached to the shoulder fringes have a clay-like material rubbed on them. The triangular flap fringe upon which the single mescalbean is strung is knotted below the mescalbean; the other fringes bearing mescalbeans are not knotted. The mescalbeans apparently have been perforated with a hot drill. All of the mescalbeans on the shoulder fringes are deep maroon in color; the mescalbean on the triangular flap fringe is a lighter red. The mescalbeans are small to medium in size, ranging from 1.0 to 1.4 cm in length and 0.8 to 1.2 cm width.

Peabody Museum of Archaeology and Ethnology, Harvard University, catalogue number 10/32710, accession number 50-69. This specimen was obtained through exchange with the Museum of the American Indian (Heye Foundation) in 1950. According to the Museum of the American Indian's catalogue information, this specimen was collected by M. R. Harrington in Oklahoma, and was accessioned in 1909. Museum of the American Indian (Heye Foundation) catalogue number 2/4365.

Specimen 46: **Pipe bag**. This specimen was on exhibit at the time of investigation, so a complete description of it was not possible. It is a buckskin bag decorated with dark blue, light blue, red, green, and white trade beads. A long fringe is attached to the bottom of the bag. A series of fringe string pairs are twisted for about one-half their length below which is strung a mescalbean and then the strings are knotted, leaving two loose ends hanging below. Not all the fringes have mescalbeans strung on them. There are approximately forty-two fringe pairs, of which only fifteen are visibly bearing mescalbeans. The fifteen mescalbeans generally are deep maroon and are relatively large, ranging from 1.3 to 1.7 cm in length and 0.9 to 1.3 cm in width.

American Museum of Natural History, catalogue number 50.1/6246, accession number not secured. Collected in 1910 by P. E. Goddard in Oklahoma.

Specimen 47: **A Peyote outfit**, including a buckskin jacket and leggings and a mescalbean necklace. The necklace consists of approximately one hundred mescalbeans. A packet containing what seems to be dried vegetal material is attached to the necklace by means of a strip of green cloth. This outfit was examined by Volney H. Jones in 1952; additional information on these specimens was not collected since it was on exhibit at the time of Professor Jones' visit.

Western Frontier Museum, Kit Carson Home, Philmont Scout Ranch, near Cimarron, New Mexico. Specimen not catalogued. According to Mr. George Bullock, Director of the Ranch in 1952, this specimen was acquired from a Mr. Kincaid of Clinton, Oklahoma.

Specimen 48: **Mescalbean necklace**, composed of fifty-one mescalbeans possibly perforated with a hot drill and strung on pink thread. The original catalogue information associated with this specimen lists "1 bean necklace with *wocowe* [peyote] bag," thereby indicating its probable association with the Peyote Religion. I have not personally examined this specimen. This description is based on catalogue information supplied by Dr. Lawrence E. Dawson, Senior Museum Anthropologist, Lowie Museum of Anthropology.

Lowie Museum of Anthropology, University of California at Berkeley, catalogue number 2-4822. Collected by Colonel H. L. Scott between 1876 and 1898. Collection locality not given.

Specimen 49: <u>Necklace</u> designed for use by a male participant in Peyote ceremonies; approximately 92 cm long. The necklace is composed primarily of two strands of spherical metal beads, 67.5 cm long. To these strings of beads is attached a rather elaborate ornament, composed of what seems to be a cloth base with two streamers to which are attached metal tacks, an eagle claw, a metal ornament, and two short strings of mescalbeans. I have not examined this specimen. The description presented here is based on a drawing and catalogue information supplied by the Denver Art Museum.

Denver Art Museum, catalogue number JKi-77-P. Purchased by Frederic H. Douglas from Mr. Charles Eagle Plume of Allenspark, Colorado. Mr. Eagle Plume acquired the necklace from a Mrs. Conn of Kingfisher, Oklahoma, whose father reportedly collected it about 1890. Accession date: July 13, 1955.

Specimen 50: <u>Peyote Religion necklace</u> composed of a single strand of mescalbeans (approximately 71 cm long) and a single strand of spherical metal beads (approximately 69 cm long). Several attachments are tied onto the string of mescalbeans: a bunch of silk ribbons, a silver crucifix, a silver button with a long string hanging from it, and a braided strand of human hair with what appears to be a beaded strip around its base above which is attached a silver button. Information on this specimen was secured through correspondence with the Denver Art Museum.

Denver Art Museum, catalogue number JKi-55-P. Purchased from J. C. Tingly of Anardarko, Oklahoma. Accession date: November 31 [sic], 1951.

Specimen 51: <u>Mescalbean necklace and peyote pouch</u> (Fig. 15). Fifty deep maroon and highly polished mescalbeans are strung on a rawhide string; the string has been broken and some of the mescalbeans presumably are missing. This mescalbean necklace is attached at several points to a light green rawhide cord, which consists of two twisted rawhide strands. A small buckskin doll is attached to the wearer's left on the necklace. The doll is dressed in a fringed buckskin dress decorated with white, navy blue, and light blue glass trade beads and small metal strips. The doll's head is crowned with "hair" made from an unidentified fuzzy white material. A light blue ribbon and the string of mescalbeans are attached by a rawhide strip to the rawhide cord behind the doll. Attached to the bottom of the necklace is a small fringed buckskin pouch, the flap of which is decorated with red, white, navy blue, light blue, and aquamarine glass trade beads. The beads are arranged in a star and circle design around a metal brad located in the center of the flap. The fringe of the pouch is decorated with single strings of white trade beads. One peyote button is enclosed and sewn inside the pouch.

Figure 15. Specimen 51: A Kiowa mescalbean necklace with a buckskin doll and peyote pouch attached. Smithsonian Institution, catalogue number 165227.

Smithsonian Institution, catalogue number 165227, accession number 26286. Collected in Oklahoma by James Mooney, probably in 1891. Accession date: October 8, 1892.

Specimen 52: <u>Mescalbean necklace</u> worn during peyote ceremonies. The specimen consists of one hundred and thirty-seven mescalbeans strung on a rawhide string. There are no attachments to the necklace except a single short piece of rawhide string knotted around the necklace between two mescalbeans. The ends of the necklace are knotted approximately 9 cm from their ends, with seven mescalbeans strung on each of the resulting appendages. Each of the ends of the string is knotted below the mescalbeans to prevent them from falling off. The necklace is 71.5 cm long (when doubled) and approximately 143 cm long when stretched out into a single strand. The mescalbeans vary widely in color from tannish-red to deep maroon. They have been perforated with a hot drill; two of the mescalbeans have been perforated through the sides instead of through the ends as is the usual practice. The majority of the seeds are medium-sized but, when the necklace is taken as a unit, the mescalbeans present range in size from 1.1 to 1.5 cm in length and 0.9 to 1.2 cm in width.

Peabody Museum of Archaeology and Ethnology, Harvard University, catalogue number 10/33517, accession number 52-27. This specimen was secured through exchange with the Denver Art Museum. According to the Denver Art Museum's catalogue information, this specimen was purchased from Mr. J. G. Tingley of Anadarko, Oklahoma. No collection date is given but the Denver Art Museum received this specimen on April 11, 1940. Denver Art Museum, catalogue number OKi-1-P.

Specimen 53: <u>Mescalbean necklace or bandoleer</u> worn during peyote ceremonies. This specimen is composed of one hundred and thirty-eight mescalbeans strung on a rawhide string. The mescalbeans vary in color from light to dark maroon, though the majority of the seeds are rather dark. They seem to have been perforated with a hot drill, but not all the mescalbeans included exhibit the discoloration associated with this method of perforation. Some of the mescalbeans are broken, presumably as a result of perforation. They all are a similar size, ranging from 1.0 to 1.3 cm in length to 0.9 to 1.2 cm in width. This string of mescalbeans is part of a peyote kit that included drumsticks, a gourd rattle, several silver peyote ornaments, and other items of peyote paraphernalia. These items are stored in a finely tooled wooden box with a metal latch and a fully beaded handle.

University Museum, University of Pennsylvania, catalogue number 59-14-55. This specimen was secured through exchange with the Denver Art Museum. According to the Denver Art Museum's catalogue information, this specimen was purchased from Mr. J. C. Tingley of Anadarko, Oklahoma, and was received by the Museum on August 21, 1941. Denver Art Museum, catalogue number OKi-2-P.

Figure 16. Specimen 55: A Kiowa "male warrior doll" (34 cm tall) wearing a mescalbean bandoleer. Smithsonian Institution, catalogue number 152918.

Specimen 54: <u>Mescalbean necklace</u>. This specimen is pictured in
Schultes (1937:Figure II). Schultes provides the following description:
"The beans (<u>Sophora</u> <u>secundiflora</u> (Orteg.) Lag. ex DC.) are strung on
buckskin. Attached to the string are several personal trinkets: a
piece of red ribbon, beaver fur, a child's ring, a lace handkerchief
with a bundle of dried beaver muscle 'medicine' under the ring. All the
necklaces are similar, but the personal trinkets vary with individual
tastes and are thought to have symbolic meaning."

Botanical Museum, Harvard University. Harvard Botanical Collection
(Economic Botany) No. 5026. Collected in July, 1936, by Richard E.
Shultes in Anadarko, Oklahoma.

Specimen 55: <u>Male warrior doll</u>, made of buckskin (Fig. 16); 34 cm
tall, 7 cm wide at the waist. The doll is dressed in a shirt, leggings
and moccasins, all made of fringed and tanned buckskin, and a breech-
cloth, made of red and white trade cloth. Bands of white trade beads
are strung on the edge of the fringe at the neck and wrists of the shirt
while bands of dark blue, light blue, and white trade beads are found
along the shoulder fringe. The upper fringe of the leggings is decorated
with light blue and white trade beads and the fringe of the moccasins
is paralleled by a band of dark blue, light blue, and yellow trade beads.
A rawhide sash serves as a belt. A painted rawhide shield with two
fringed strips of buckskin trailing from behind is attached to the doll's
left arm. The shield is decorated with a blue dot in the center with
blue, yellow, and red lines drawn across the entire circumference of the
shield below the central blue dot and a series of small blue dots arranged along the edge of the shield above the central blue dot. In addition, two leather cut-outs in the shape of bear paws are attached to the
front of the shield. The face of the doll is drawn in. The doll's hair
is light brown and is braided on the sides and in the back. The side
braids are wrapped in cloth. The doll is wearing a mescalbean bandoleer
over its left shoulder and under its right arm; this arrangement is not
necessarily original since the bandoleer can be removed from the doll.
The bandoleer is 20 cm long and is composed of thirty perforated mescalbeans strung on a thin rawhide string. The majority of the mescalbeans
are of a deep maroon color while the remainder are of a lighter red color.
None of the mescalbeans are discolored around their perforations, indicating perhaps that they were perforated with a cold drill. The seeds
vary slightly in size, the largest approximately 1.5 cm long, the shortest approximately 1 cm long. Although most of the seeds are ovoid in
shape, some have flat ends, indicating that they were not as carefully
selected for uniformity as the seeds of other specimens examined.

Smithsonian Institution, catalogue number 152918, accession number 25718.
Collected in Indian Territory by James Mooney in 1891. Accession date:
September, 1891.

Figure 17. Setûñtekûñ or War Bonnet, a Kiowa-Apache, wearing a mescalbean bandoleer and a Sophora secundiflora pod attached to the right shoulder fringe of his shirt. Photograph taken by DeLancey Gill in 1913. Reproduced courtesy of the National Anthropological Archives, Smithsonian Institution (negative number 2598-C).

Kiowa-Apache

There is no indication that the Kiowa-Apache ever employed mescalbeans for any purposes other than as seed beads. Parsons (1941:36, 36n. 108) reports that a Kiowa-Apache doctor wore a mescalbean necklace when curing a Caddo child. He performed this cure sometime after the beginning of the reservation period. Powers (1972:164) reproduces a photograph of a young Kiowa-Apache woman wearing a buckskin dress with what seem to be mescalbeans attached to strings looped through the front of the dress at bust level (National Anthropological Archives, Smithsonian Institution, negative number 2600-B). I also have examined photographs in the National Anthropological Archives (negative numbers 2598-A and C) of a Kiowa-Apache man with a mescalbean pod attached to the long shoulder fringe of his buckskin shirt (Fig. 17).

Mandan

Howard (n.d.) reports that the Mandan formerly wore mescalbean bandoleers as items of Peyote Religion paraphernalia. Additional information on Mandan use of mescalbeans, either published or in the form of museum specimens, is wanting.

Missouri

It is very likely that the Missouri participated in mescalbean medicine society ceremonialism during the pre-reservation period in view of the fact that after 1830 they were closely affiliated with the Oto who maintained such a society. However, information regarding Missouri use of mescalbeans is restricted to the far from satisfactory data supplied below.

Specimen 56: "Red Medicine War Necklace." This specimen was not examined since it could not be located at the time of the investigation. However, the name given it on the catalogue card suggests that it is a mescalbean necklace.

Museum of the American Indian (Heye Foundation), catalogue number 3/3690. Collected by M. R. Harrington in Oklahoma. No collection date given. Accession date: between 1913 and 1923.

Ojibwa

Howard (n.d.) notes that mescalbean bandoleers formerly were worn by participants in Ojibwa peyote ceremonies performed in Cass Lake, Minnesota, and that some Ojibwa members of this community have, in recent times, consumed mescalbeans "for experiment." I have examined a photograph of an Ojibwa baby in a "Western-type" cradle to which are attached what appear to be mescalbeans. I have not secured the date and location at which this photograph was taken. It is the property of the Marquette County Historical Society and appears on the inside back cover of Michigan Commission on Indian Affairs (n.d.). No additional information on the use of mescalbeans by the Ojibwa has come to my attention. No museum specimens of mescalbeans of Ojibwa provenience were located during the investigation.

Omaha

The Omaha maintained a "Wichita Dance" or "Red Medicine Society," but the members apparently did not consume mescalbeans. Instead, initiates were "shot" with "red medicine" (presumably mescalbeans) on the fourth day

Figure 18. Specimen 57: An Omaha girl's hair ornament composed of glass and metal beads, mescalbeans, and two shells strung on a buckskin thong. American Museum of Natural History, catalogue number 50.2/3104.

of their initiation into the society (Dorsey 1884:349-50); Gilmore 1924: 62). In addition, Dorsey (1884:349-50) reports that the members of this society, which included at least one woman, had a medicine (not identified but probably mescalbeans) that they rubbed on their bodies and bullets prior to battles (presumably to harden both) and that they administered to their horses before engaging in a buffalo surround. Howard (1957:80) reports that each member of this society had at least one mescalbean in his or her personal medicine bundle. Dorsey (1884:350) states that what appear to have been mescalbean packets were attached to a medicine string, worn in bandoleer fashion over the left shoulder and under the right arm, during the performances of the Omaha Red Medicine Society. More recently, Gilmore (1938: personal communication to Volney H. Jones) relates that the Omaha wrap mescalbeans in buckskin packets which are slit so that the beans can see out. These are attached by a thong to articles of clothing or other objects as charms or fetishes. One modern use is to attach such packets to the coat lapel of a person starting out on a journey to make his trip successful. Similarly, Dorsey (1894:416) reports from the late nineteenth century that what seem to have been mescalbeans were believed by the Omaha to bestow good luck on their owners (cf. Gilmore 1919:99). In 1953, Howard (n.d.) observed dancers in the Omaha equivalent of the Grass Dance wearing mescalbean bandoleers and learned that until recently such bandoleers also were worn by Omaha peyotists.

Specimen 57: <u>Girl's hair ornament</u> (Fig. 18), 35.5 cm long. This ornament is composed of two shells, ten mescalbeans, nineteen silver metal beads, and ten black faceted glass beads strung on commercial cotton string. These components are arranged in the following pattern: a shell is strung on each end of the string between which are several sets of two silver metal beads separated by a black faceted glass bead. These sets in turn are separated by a mescalbean on either end. A buckskin thong is tied about midway in the string for attachment to "the back of a little girl's joined braids." All of the ten mescalbeans present are of a more or less uniform dark brownish-red color. They all have been perforated with a hot drill and two are cracked as a result. They vary in size from 1.2 to 1.5 cm in length and 1.0 to 1.3 cm in width.

American Museum of Natural History, catalogue number 50.2/3104, accession number 1930-44. Collected in the summer of 1930 by Margaret Mead in Nebraska. Accession date: 1930.

Specimen 58: Personal medicine bundle of Teoka^{n}ha, an Omaha man born in 1833. This bundle and certain of its contents are pictured and described by Gilmore (1924). According to Gilmore, the bundle is divided into four units: "(1) an emblem of the revelation and gift of power granted to Teoka^{n}ha at his puberty fast; (2) the emblem of a revelation and gift of power granted to him in the prime of his manhood as a free favor from the buffalo, and not as a reward of fasting; (3) Teoka^{n}ha's war bundle, which he had by inheritance from his father; (4) emblems of the Wichita Society, or 'Red Medicine Society,' of which Teoka^{n}ha was a member." Of particular interest here are the first and last of these units. The first unit contains a jackrabbit skin, since the jackrabbit became Teoka^{n}ha's "personal patron and guardian spirit." Two perforated mescalbeans are attached by a buckskin thong to the skin just below the head. The Red Medicine Society unit of the bundle contains "eight strands of sweetgrass (Savastana odorata)," a cane whistle with wavy lines cut into its surface, and a buckskin packet containing two seeds. Gilmore identified these two seeds as Erythrina flabelliformis, but one has subsequently been reidentified as Sophora secundiflora by Volney H. Jones. I examined this bundle during the period of investigation and determined that the second seed included in this packet is that of Abrus precatorius L.

Museum of the American Indian (Heye Foundation), catalogue number 12/6225. Collected by Melvin Gilmore in 1923 from George Ramsay, Teoka^{n}ha's son, of Walthill, Nebraska. Accession date: 1929.

Osage

Dorsey (1884:351n. 21) relates that the Osage maintained a "Red Medicine Dance," presumably a local example of the mescalbean medicine society. He also suggests that the "Red Medicine" (apparently mescalbeans) of this society was employed as a fetish (Dorsey 1894:416). He provides no additional information regarding the use of mescalbeans by the members of this society, adding only that its leader was a man. Howard (n.d.) reports that contemporary Osage employ mescalbean bandoleers in their full dress and dance costumes. A photograph of mescalbean bandoleers being worn in a modern day Osage dance can be found in Churchill (1946:23). In addition, numerous photographs of Osage men wearing mescalbean necklaces and bandoleers are housed in the collections of the National Anthropological Archives, Smithsonian Institution (for example, negative numbers 4121-A and B; 4129-A; 4132-A and B; 4137-B-1, 2, and 3; 4148-B; 4151, 4155-A; 4159-A; and 54962). At least one of these Osage bandoleers includes coralbeans (negative number 4066-B).

Specimen 59: "Sacred bean from Osage Indians." This specimen consists of a single perforated mescalbean collected at the Tewa Pueblo of Santa Clara in 1910 by Mrs. Blanche Trask. In the catalogue information accompanying this specimen, Mrs. Trask states that beans of this kind were obtained by the inhabitants of Santa Clara Pueblo in exchange with the Osage. She fails to report how either the Santa Clara or Osage Indians used them. I have not examined this specimen. Dr. Lawrence E. Dawson, Senior Museum Anthropologist, Lowie Museum of Anthropology, provided the information related above and attests to the identification of the seed as Sophora secundiflora.

Lowie Museum of Anthropology, University of California at Berkeley, catalogue number 2-9873.

Oto

The members of the Oto Red Bean Medicine Lodge consumed an emetic and perhaps stimulating decoction of mescalbeans during the performance of their ceremonies (James 1905, vol. 16:216-17; Whitman 1937:120-21). In addition, Howard (1957:81) learned that Oto peyotists had at one time mixed mescalbeans and peyote for consumption. Dorsey (1894:416) reports in the late nineteenth century that what seem to have been mescalbeans were carried by Oto individuals--probably both males and females--apparently to bring them good luck. More recently, mescalbean bandoleers have become popular items in contemporary Oto dance costumes (Howard n.d.).

Specimen 60: "Charm or medicine necklace," pictured and described by Alanson Skinner (1925:36-38). The basic component of this necklace is a military shoulder ornament which has been wrapped with yellow and red dyed porcupine quills near the metal pendants at its ends. The rest of the ornament is covered with "a wrapping of coarse 'pony trader' beads in alternate bands of white and blue." Attached to this foundation are two perforated grizzly-bear claws, the "dried hand of an Indian child, with thumb and fingers outspread," a portion of a human scalp, "a small deer-skin packet containing two coral beans (Erythrina flabelliformis), and a thimble containing a packet of scarlet powder." This specimen was examined in 1946 by Volney H. Jones, who reidentified the "two coral beans" as unusually small seeds of Sophora secundiflora.

Museum of the American Indian (Heye Foundation). Catalogue number, accession number and date, and collection information were not located during the period of investigation.

Specimen 61: Red medicine bundle. A piece of red cotton trade cloth with floral designs serves as the outer wrapping of this bundle. Inside is (1) what seems to be an incomplete (i.e., unbored) two-jointed cane flute, 47.5 cm long and 2 cm in diameter; (2) a circular piece of wood, 4 cm in diameter with a star carved in bas-relief on it--apparently an ink stamp since faint traces of ink are found on the star--wrapped in a gray cotton cloth with floral designs tied up with a cotton string; (3) a white trade cloth wrapper containing (a) one kit fox skin, 74 cm long with reddish and brownish gray fur and no attachments; and (b) a wooden flute, 34 cm long and 2.5 cm in diameter, with a rectangular air hole and a stopper apparently made of clay. White clay is rubbed all over the exterior of the flute and four strands of cotton cord are tied to the flute just above the air hole. A bunch of unidentified feathers are attached with a rawhide string to the top of the flute. At the top of the bunch of feathers is inserted a tanned leather packet containing what appear to be two mescalbeans (the identification of these seeds is not positive since the seed scars are not visible). The packet is wrapped very tightly around the seeds and is perforated around the seeds at the top. The packet is smeared with white clay.

Museum of the American Indian (Heye Foundation), catalogue number 3/3661. Collected in Oklahoma by M. R. Harrington. No collection date given but presumably collected in December, 1912 (Harrington 1913:107-108). Accession date: 1913.

Specimen 62: <u>Red Medicine Society bundle</u>. This bundle consists of a calico wrapper containing the following items: (1) Two unidentified animal skins. (2) A bunch of unidentified feathers wrapped in trade cloth, 22 cm long. (3) A bunch of feathers (possibly hawk) wrapped at their base with strips of rawhide and blue trade cloth. A cotton cord is wound around this packet of feathers and its two ends are knotted. This packet is 31 cm long excluding the cotton cord. (4) Five single-jointed cane flutes, one undecorated, the remaining four with wavy lines cut into their surface. Of these four, one flute is incomplete (one end is not perforated) and a second has white clay rubbed on it. Another of these four decorated flutes is long and slender and bears several attachments: a bunch of unidentified feathers is tied to one end of the flute; a horn-like substance with three rawhide strands hanging from it is attached to the flute just above the sound hole; and a single <u>Sophora secundiflora</u> pod containing two mescalbeans is tied onto the flute by a rawhide string. (5) A poorly preserved strip of fur (26 cm long and 2.5 - 3.0 cm wide) with a deer tail and a perforated leather packet tightly wrapped around two mescalbeans at one end and a similar packet containing what seem to be mescalbeans (their seed scars are not visible) at the other end. (6) A string of cotton cord (52 cm long doubled) bearing six leather packets tightly wrapped around at least two different kinds of seeds. The seeds are missing from two of these packets. Of the remaining four packets, two contain what seem to be mescalbeans (hilum not visible), another contains two mescalbeans, and the last holds four spherical black seeds which are unidentified but which definitely are not mescalbeans.

Museum of the American Indian (Heye Foundation), catalogue number 3/3662. Collected in Oklahoma by M. R. Harrington. No collection date given but presumably collected in December, 1912 (Harrington 1913:107-08). Accession date: 1913.

Specimen 63: <u>Red Medicine Bundle</u>. A calico wrapper with paisley-like designs contains the following items: (1) Several strands of red and purple wool yarn braided together. (2) An unidentified animal skin. (3) A bunch of feathers --possibly hawk--(32 cm long). (4) A bunch of buffalo wool. (5) An unidentified fur "trailer" (133 cm long and 8 cm wide) folded in half, wrapped with red felt strouding at intervals, and bearing an imitation eagle claw attached by a black ribbon, a bunch of small yellow feathers at one end, and a bunch of hawk-like feathers at the other. A small rawhide packet containing two mescalbeans is attached at the base of the hawk feathers. The packet is perforated, exposing portions of the mescalbeans to view. (6) A one-jointed cane flute (28 cm long, 2.2 cm in diameter) with a rectangular sound hole and a stopper possibly of clay. Four parallel wavy lines are cut into the surface of the flute, extending for the majority of its length. White clay has been smeared into these grooves. Rawhide strings attach a perforated rawhide packet containing what appears to be one mescalbean (hilum not visible) to one end of the flute. A rawhide cord composed of two twisted rawhide strands is designed to suspend the flute around the wearer's neck. A hole is bored in the opposite end of the flute through which passes another rawhide cord which bears a cut eagle feather (31 cm long).

Museum of the American Indian (Heye Foundation), catalogue number 3/3673. Collected in Oklahoma by M. R. Harrington, apparently in December, 1912 (Harrington 1913:107-08). Accession date: 1913.

Pawnee

Among the Pawnee, a decoction of mescalbeans apparently was consumed only by initiates of the Pawnee Deer Society at the time of their induction to induce an unconscious state (Murie 1914:605-08); Densmore 1929:47). The members of this Deer Society also manipulated mescalbeans in sleight-of-hand during performances of their Deer Dance (Murie 1914: 605-06; Weltfish 1965:386-402). La Barre (1969:106) reports that the Pawnee formerly ingested mescalbeans "to strengthen the body," and Howard (n.d.) states that modern day Pawnee individuals wear mescalbean bandoleers in both peyote and non-peyote contexts. In addition, Garland Blaine (1976: personal communication) informs me that Pawnee women have worn mescalbean chokers during portions of the twentieth century.

Specimen 64: Two paint bags with two mescalbeans attached to each end of the two tie strings on each bag. A total of four mescalbeans are attached to each bag. I have not examined this specimen personally, but Volney H. Jones did so in 1933.

Field Museum of Natural History, catalogue number 71639 and 71642. Collected in 1902 by George A. Dorsey, presumably in Oklahoma.

Specimen 65: Mescalbean necklace, 96 cm long (single strand). This necklace consists of thirty-five mescalbeans strung on a rawhide cord. The two ends of the rawhide string extend beyond the mescalbeans for tying around the wearer's neck. Most of the mescalbeans are a dull reddish-brown while others are more maroon. All have been perforated with a hot drill, and as a result, a number are cracked and wrinkled. They range in size from 1.0 to 1.5 cm in length and 0.8 to 1.2 cm in width.

American Museum of Natural History, catalogue number 50.1/167, accession number 1910-18. No collector or collection date and locality given. This specimen, at one time included in the Emil W. Lenders Collection, was donated to the American Museum of Natural History by J. P. Morgan. Accession date: 1910.

Specimen 66: <u>String of mescalbeans</u>. The string is broken in several places so an exact measurement of it cannot be made; however it appears to have been rather short originally, perhaps 27 cm or less in length, which suggests that it may have been worn around the wrist or ankle rather than around the neck. The twenty mescalbeans are strung on two strands of thin cotton fishing line-type cord and the two ends apparently were knotted together. The mescalbeans vary considerably in color from tannish-red to deep maroon. They were perforated rather crudely with a hot drill and many of the seeds are wrinkled and cracked as a result. They range in size from 1.0 to 1.5 cm in length and from 0.8 to 1.1 cm in width.

American Museum of Natural History, catalogue number 50.1/137, accession numbers 1910-18. No collector, collection date, or locality given. This specimen, once a part of the Emil W. Lenders Collections, was donated to the American Museum of Natural History by J. P. Morgan. Accession date: 1910.

Specimen 67: <u>Deer Society Bundle</u>. The outside wrapper of this bundle is a 48-star American flag (145 by 96 cm). This bundle contains the following items: (1) One skin (probably red fox), 96 cm long from the tip of the nose to the tip of the tail and 28 cm wide at the shoulders. Three bunches of feathers are attached with rawhide strings to the skin. The first bunch consists of eight feathers (possibly hawk) attached at the shoulders; the second consists of six similar feathers attached about midway down the back; the third consists of four eagle feathers attached near the tail. (2) A reddish and gray fur skin (perhaps a coyote skin) 110 cm long from the tip of the nose to the tip of the tail and 24 cm wide at the shoulders. A human scalp is attached to the top of the head and, immediately behind the scalp, is a bunch of three eagle feathers. About midway down the back is a bunch of six feathers (possibly hawk). A third bunch of eight similar feathers is found near the tail. All the feathers in these three bunches are wrapped at their bases with sinew, which connects them to rawhide strings which in turn serve to attach the bunches of feathers to the skin. (3) A complete deer tail, 17 cm long, with two buckskin tie strings attached, apparently employed as a dance ornament worn around the waist and falling down to the buttocks of the wearer. (4) A buffalo hair rope, 124 cm long, whose ends have been tied together apparently for use as a bandoleer. Several eagle feathers are attached to this rope by rawhide strings which pass through perforations in the base of the feathers. The end of the quill of each feather is cut off flat. (5) Several feathers (perhaps hawk) with

Figure 19. Specimen 67: A snapping turtle paw bag included in a Pawnee Deer Society bundle. The bag contains a peyote button wrapped in buckskin, a mescalbean, a plum pit die, and a piece of deer tail. American Museum of Natural History, catalogue number 50.1/8486.

small red-dyed feathers attached to their tops and their bases wrapped with sinew to form a bunch which then is wrapped onto a pointed stick (ca. 42 cm long). The result is very similar to the prayer plumes employed by Native American groups in the American Southwest. (6) An undecorated cane whistle, 33.2 cm long. (7) A small buckskin bag (8 by 5 cm) containing three dice apparently prepared from plum pits. (8) A clawed snapping turtle paw bag (Fig. 19). The white portion of a deer's tail is stuffed into the top of the paw bag. The bag contains one plum pit die and the only mescalbean found in this bundle (it is medium red in color and measures 1.7 by 1.2 cm). The die and mescalbean are resting on a strip of buckskin, which is wrapped around a small peyote button (Lophophora williamsii), 2.5 cm in diameter.

American Museum of Natural History, catalogue number 50.1/8486, accession number 1915-62. Collected by James R. Murie in Oklahoma; no collection date given. Accession dates: September 30, 1915 and October 20, 1915.

Ponca

Howard (1965:122-23) reports that the members of the Ponca mescalbean medicine society consumed a decoction of mescalbeans which sometimes produced visions and that the Ponca occasionally gave their horses and mules a mescalbean tea "to make them swift and to cure their infirmities." Howard (1962:133, n.d.) also learned that mescalbeans were shot as "medicine arrows" during the performances of the Ponca Medicine Lodge ceremonies. The Ponca employed mescalbeans as charms to insure success in hunting and apparently to bring good luck in general (Howard 1965:123, n.d.). Ponca warriors formerly carried perforated buckskin packets of mescalbeans or placed a mescalbean in either ear for protection during raiding expeditions. Using mescalbeans as charms seems to have been practiced by both members and non-members of the Ponca mescalbean medicine society (Howard 1965:123, n.d.; Whitman 1939:192). In addition, mescalbean bandoleer and bracelets were worn by the members of one of the Ponca warrior dancing societies during the performance of their ceremonies, and mescalbean bandoleers have been donned by Ponca peyotists during peyote meetings (Howard n.d.). Powers (1972: frontispiece) reproduces a 1914 photograph of Standing Elk, a Ponca, wearing three mescalbean bandoleers over his left shoulder and under his right arm (National Anthropological Archives, Smithsonian Institution, negative number 4227). Ponca men wearing similar bandoleers appear in several photographs housed in the collections of the National Anthropological Archives (negative numbers 4215; 4217-A and B; 4218-A and B; and 4222-C). Howard (n.d.) also reports that the buckskin costume of the father of one of his Northern Ponca informants was decorated with mescalbeans; I have examined photographs of a Ponca man wearing a buckskin shirt with mescalbeans strung on the leather strings that are looped through the front of the shirt (National Anthropological Archives, negative numbers 4226-A and B). Other photographs in the same collection (negative numbers 4220-A and B) depict a Ponca man wearing a hair ornament composed of a feather base and strings of both mescalbeans and what appear to be small spherical metal beads.

Specimen 68: <u>Beaded pouch</u>, consisting of a beaded cloth front and an undecorated, finely tanned, leather back; 25.7 cm long, 19.5 cm wide at the top, 16.8 cm wide at the bottom. The cloth front is completely beaded with strings of red, blue, pink, white, green, yellow, and black trade beads. The central design is an inner circle of white beads dissected by a blue cross, surrounded by a circle of alternating red and white triangles. Horizontal bars of alternating green and white beads run from the top to the bottom of the pouch with vertical bars of red, blue, black, pink, and white beads arranged in a row across the top. A triangle of yellow beads with a narrow vertical bar of blue beads to the interior of the pouch is found at each of the bottom corners. A tanned white leather thong is attached to each side of the top of the pouch; these thongs are tied together to form a handle. Two tanned white leather thongs are attached to the top center of the front of the pouch, with two mescalbeans strung on each. A similar leather string is looped through the side of the pouch near each of the four corners. Two mescalbeans are strung on each of the two ends of these strings, except at the lower right hand corner where only one end is present, the other apparently having been broken off. This specimen bears a total of eighteen mescalbeans, all of which apparently were perforated with a hot drill. They are all of a uniform medium red color and of the same general size, approximately 1.0 cm wide and ranging in length from 0.8 to 1.5 cm.

Smithsonian Institution, catalogue number 357753, accession number 113605. Collected in Oklahoma, no date. Acquired by bequest from the Estate of Victor J. Evans. Accession date: March 26, 1931.

Prairie Potawatomi

Skinner (1924-27:231-32) reports that the Prairie Potawatomi consumed a decoction of mescalbeans in the context of their "Throwing-Out-Medicine Ceremony," but he fails to relate for what purposes this decoction was consumed or what effects it produced in the individuals who consumed it. Howard (1962) recently secured additional information on the Prairie Potawatomi use of mescalbeans in ritual contexts and learned that Prairie Potawatomi warriors formerly carried mescalbeans on raiding expeditions as war medicine. According to Howard (1962:130) these warriors "took the bean either in dry powder form or as a tea before going into battle. This gave them courage and superhuman strength. Warriors also used an infusion of the bean to wash out and sterilize their battle wounds." Howard (1962:131) also examined a necklace made from forty-six mescalbeans and forty-one elk teeth. The mescalbeans served as spacers between the elk teeth, with three mescalbeans placed together on each end of the string. The necklace is reported to date from the "period of tribal warfare." Howard (1962:131) learned that the Prairie Potowatomi also wore mescalbean bracelets around their wrists as a "protective

Figure 20. Mescalbeans at Taos Pueblo. The boy on the right wears a double bandoleer of mescalbeans. The bandoleer as well as some of the other items of clothing worn by the individuals pictured here indicate Southern Plains influence. Photograph taken between 1900 and 1920 by an unidentified photographer. Reproduced courtesy of the National Anthropological Archives, Smithsonian Institution (negative number 4591).

fetish." Mescalbean bandoleers are worn by Prairie Potawatomi peyotists, and individual mescalbeans have been attached, in recent times at least, to the fringe of buckskin shirts, leggings, and dresses. No specimens of mescalbeans attributable to the Prairie Potawatomi were located during the period of investigation.

Pueblos

There is very little indication that any of the Pueblo groups ever employed mescalbeans for any purpose. A single perforated mescalbean collected at Santa Clara Pueblo perhaps was secured in trade from the Osage, but there is no report indicating how it might have been employed at Santa Clara. It is described here as specimen 59 in the section discussing Osage mescalbean use. The only other evidence of the presence of mescalbeans among Pueblo groups is a photograph of a boy at Taos Pueblo wearing a mescalbean bandoleer (National Anthropological Archives, Smithsonian Institution, negative number 4591). This photograph is reproduced here as Figure 20.

Sac and Fox

Information regarding the use of mescalbeans by the Sac and Fox is restricted to that secured in connection with the museum specimens described below.

Specimen 69: <u>Good-Will Bundle</u>, "used in promoting friendship between the Sac and Fox and other tribes." This bundle is described by M. R. Harrington (1914:239-41) as follows:
> The outer cover of the bundle was a woven sack, 12 1/2" x 9 1/2", made of a black yarn resembling buffalo wool and ravelings of three colors, red, green, and yellow.

Contents.--An unusually fine woven bead work sack with patterns in nine different colors and shades, size 6 3/4" x 4 3/8". It enclosed: An imitation bear claw made of horn, with two perforations; a woven sack of blanket ravelings, pale green and red, 4 1/2" x 4", in which were three pieces of some rough root and three others recognized as calamus, a double package containing in one side some small roots and brownish flat seeds, in the other a few very small seeds, black and lustrous, a brass thimble containing a buckskin packet of friendship or love medicine, and a package of roots. A smaller woven sack seemingly of buffalo wool, ravelings and fibre (Indian hemp?), was also found in the beadwork pouch, and yielded a tiny packet of red magic paint, a package of finely divided mineral substance with glistening specks resembling mica, another of slender black roots, and a slim bead of shell resembling wampum, but twice the length. All the preceding were stored in the bead sack.

Woven sack, 3 1/2" x 4 3/4", mainly of buffalo wool and (Indian hemp?), contains a cloth package of pieces of root and a mixture of pounded herbs wrapped in a fragment of a Washington newspaper of the year 1860; five little packets of cloth and paper enclosing herbs and roots, one of them yielding also a packet of magic paint; a pouch of red trade cloth, itself containing two spherical objects, one gray, one white, resembling marbles; a long purple shell bead of the variety known as "Dutch wampum;" a red mescal bean; a package of herb mixture; a wad of light hair from some animal, perhaps a white buffalo; a package of mica-like substance wrapped in a strip of red and a strip of blue calico; some whitish earthy substance done up in calico; three cloth and paper packages herbs and roots; and three loose pieces of root.

Cloth sack containing two buckskin packets herb medicine, an empty thimble and fourteen oval glass beads.

Two cloth packages containing vegetable medicines-- roots, barks, and seeds.

This bundle was not examined during the period of investigation.

Museum of the American Indian (Heye Foundation), catalogue number 2/6379. Collected by M. R. Harrington from Kī ma wa tä pä, a Sac and Fox of Oklahoma. No collection date given. Accession date: between 1910 and 1913.

Specimen 70: "Medicine doll bundle," described by M. R. Harrington (1914:236-37). The contents of the bundle were kept in a calico bag, wrapped in a piece of red calico. The central item in the bundle is a
> figure of a man, a little less than 9 1/4" high, made of hard wood, apparently oak, and dressed in a red calico shirt, red breech clout and buckskin leggings and moccasins. Across the left shoulder was a broad bead work sash, and from the ears hung long white glass beads. Directly about the fetish was a piece of blue woolen cloth. In the bundle also were a small wooden feast bowl and spoon, an old tattered mink skin painted red on the flesh side, a small blue cloth wallet decorated with ribbon appliqué containing four red mescal beans, a lot of bits of roots and herbs, and two shoulder blades of some small aminal; and an old beaded cloth pouch enclosing the tail of a small weasel and a yellow feather.

This specimen was not examined during the period of investigation.

Museum of the American Indian (Heye Foundation), catalogue number 2/7161. Purchased by M. R. Harrington from Pem wän ta, a Sac-Fox of Oklahoma. No collection date given. Accession date: between 1910 and 1913.

Specimen 71: Fox mescalbean necklace with bear claws and a muskrat skin bag attached; 89 cm long (doubled). In the catalogue information accompanying this specimen, it is described as a "Love charm" for use by a young man. The specimen consists of two strings of mescalbeans strung on tanned leather thongs. The two strings are not attached to one another except at the bottom of the necklace where the two ends of each string are attached to the opposite sides of the top of a muskrat skin bag. The end of the mescalbean strings extend along the side of the bag and are knotted at their ends. A bear claw is attached to the ends of one of the two mescalbean strings so that one bear claw is found on each side of the bag. The skin bag apparently was entirely covered with fur at one time but at present much of the fur has fallen off. The flap of the bag is secured by a rawhide string attached to the flap, which is tied to a string in the center of the bag. Rawhide strings are attached to the base of the bag and bear metal tinklers with dyed orange horsehair inside. The bag measured 7.5 cm by 7.5 cm without the tinklers and 11 cm by 7.5 cm with the tinklers. The bag contains two bunches of red ribbons, one composed of three ribbons, the other of four. The ribbons are pushed into two brass thimbles to form a pendant. A packet of trade cloth tied with commercial cotton cord and containing a flattened bunch of unidentified vegetal material is rolled up in the three-ribbon thimble pendant. There are two hundred and seventy-four mescalbeans in this specimen. They are generally of the same color, all a light brownish-red tint rather than the deep maroon often characteristic of such specimens. They vary considerably in shape and size, ranging from 1.0 to 1.5 cm in length and 0.8 to 1.1 cm in width.

Museum of the American Indian (Heye Foundation), catalogue number 16/6897. Collected in 1929 by George G. Heye from George Y. Bear of Tama, Iowa. Accession date: 1929.

Specimen 72: <u>Fox general medicine bundle</u>, described in detail by M. R. Harrington (1914:221-23). According to Harrington: "The cover is an unusually handsome and perfect woven sack, 15" x 9 3/8", largely of native materials, such as Indian hemp and buffalo wool yarn. The design on one side represents eight long-tailed monsters or 'dream panthers'; on each end, 4 1/2 human figures. The remainder of the specimen was covered with geometric designs, especially fine in form and color."

The bundle contains five categories of components divided according to intended use: love medicine, gambling medicine, curing medicine, medicine for footracing, and medicine for protection from witches. The first three categories consist of several packages of vegetal materials. The footracing medicine, according to Harrington, "consists of the tail of a newborn colt to tie on the hair for power and endurance in running, two rabbits' feet to tie on the necklace for speed, a pawpaw seed to hold in the mouth, and two cylindrical magic stones, one of them artifically shaped, to hold in the hands while running." The medicines against witches also include packets of vegetal materials and two necklaces, one of beads, the other of horsehair. Of the latter, Harrington remarks: "A necklace of horsehair, braided into the form of a square sennit and decorated with strips of otter fur bore a cloth packet containing a wampum bead and two red 'mescal' beans, Mes kwī na da wī nōn, and a buckskin packet, containing another similar bean, the whole forming a protective amulet against witches." This specimen was not examined during the period of investigation.

Museum of the American Indian (Heye Foundation), catalogue number 2/8598. Collected by M. R. Harrington from Jim Mamesa, a Fox of Tama, Iowa. No collection date given. Accession date: between 1910 and 1913.

Specimen 73: <u>A Fox amulet</u>, described by M. R. Harrington (1914:251) as follows: "This small amulet, for general good luck, consists of three red 'mescal' beans in a tight buckskin packet, with a round hole cut over each bean so that it can 'look out.' Such amulets, I was told, could be worn attached to the hair or clothing, but nowadays are usually carried in the pocket. The Fox name is Mes kwī na dá wī non, or Red medicine." This specimen could not be located at the time of the investigation.

Museum of the American Indian (Heye Foundation), catalogue number 2/8021. Collected by M. R. Harrington from members of the Fox band living near Tama, Iowa. No collection date given. Accession date: between 1910 and 1913.

Shawnee

Voegelin (n.d.) reports that the Oklahoma Shawnee wore mescalbean necklaces during the performances of their Warrior's or Man's Dance held in August. When not in use, these necklaces were stored in a bundle. Voegelin (n.d.; cf. La Barre 1969:109) also collected a semi-legendary account of how a Shawnee youth was given a mescalbean by his grandfather to carry with him for protection on raiding expeditions. There is no indication that the Shawnee ever consumed mescalbeans or that they maintained a mescalbean medicine society. Nor is there any conclusive evidence that the Shawnee were familiar with mescalbeans prior to their arrival west of the Mississippi. John Tanner (1956:144-46) reports that an Ojibwa Indian proselytizing the message of the Shawnee Prophet (the brother of Tecumseh) possessed four strings of "mouldy and discoloured beans," which were said to be made of the flesh of the Prophet. Converts fondled the strings of beans like rosaries to indicate their acceptance of the Prophet's message. This act was called "shaking hands with the prophet." La Barre (1972:300-301) identifies these beans as Sophora secundiflora, but I have been unable to locate any primary sources of information that reveal their identity. No museum specimens of mescalbeans of Shawnee provenience were discovered during this investigation.

Shoshone and Northern Ute

I have not discovered any published information definitely indicating the use of mescalbeans by any Shoshone or Northern Ute bands. Densmore (1922:130) relates that a Northern Ute doctor obtained from the Shoshone

Figure 21a. Specimen 74: A Shoshone shirt with mescalbeans attached to the shoulder and sleeve fringe. Smithsonian Institution, catalogue number 357503.

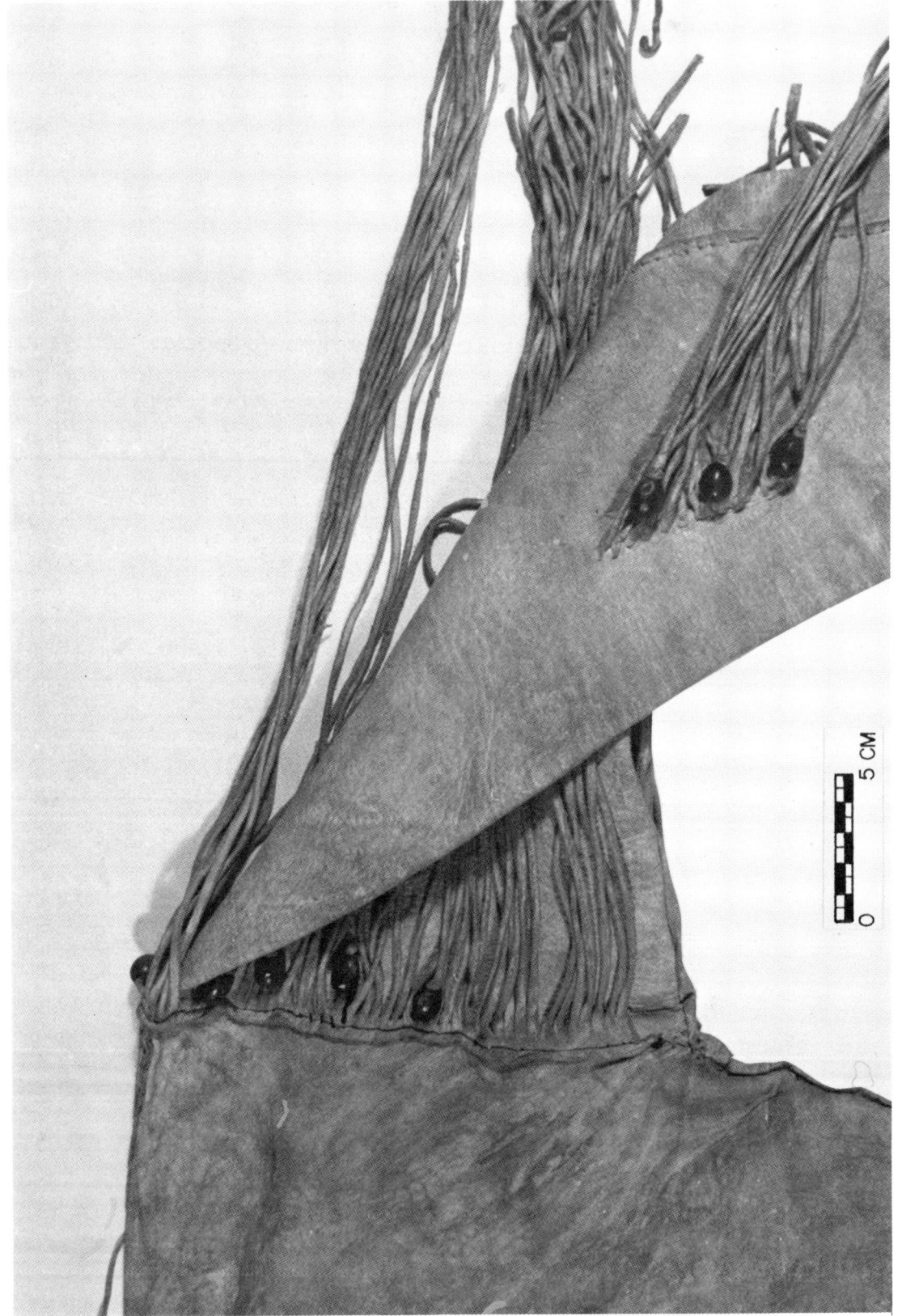

Figure 21b. An enlarged view of the shoulder and sleeve portions of the same specimen.

a highly valued plant, the powdered root of which she employed as a medicament in curing very ill patients. According to Densmore, the doctor "also had 'three little round things,' which were part of the plant. These were said to resemble a walnut but were smoother than a walnut and red in color. They were pierced with a hole so that they resembled large beads. The sick person was required to place one of these in his mouth and 'draw air through the hole.'" This description of "little round things" immediately suggests the seeds of Sophora secundiflora or Erythrina flabelliformis. However, it is unlikely that the roots of either of these two plants would have been available to the Shoshone or Northern Ute. If the root and the "little round things" were in fact from the same plant, then the "little round things" probably were not mescalbeans or E. flabelliformis seeds.

Specimen 74: Shoshone man's tanned buckskin shirt (Fig. 21), 75 cm long, 56 cm wide at the shoulders. The bottom of the shirt and the bottoms of the sleeves are cut into fringes. A number of tanned leather strings are looped through the front and back sides of the shirt at the breast, to some of which are attached red and blue ribbons. Deeply fringed triangular pieces of leather are sewn to the neck of the shirt, front and back. In addition, deeply fringed strips of leather are attached to the shoulders and the back side of each sleeve. Mescalbeans are strung on several of the fringes at the shoulder (seven mescalbeans at the right shoulder, eight at the left) and several on the fringe at the back side of the sleeves (three on each sleeve), bringing the total number of mescalbeans on this specimen to twenty-two. The mescalbeans range in color from light to dark maroon. They are all of a generally uniform medium size, but no exact measurement of them were taken, nor was the method of perforation determined.

Smithsonian Institution, catalogue number 357503, accession number 113605. No collection date or locality given. Acquired by bequest from the Estate of Victor J. Evans. Accession date: March 26, 1931.

Figure 22. A Brule man wearing a doubled string of mescalbeans as a hair ornament. Photograph probably taken at the St. Louis World's Fair in 1904 by an unidentified photographer. Reproduced courtesy of the National Anthropological Archives, Smithsonian Institution (negative number 15805).

Sioux

Riggs (1893:227-29) reports that a "mysterious bean or shell" was extracted from initiates after apparently having been shot into them during the performance of the Dakota "Mystery Dance," a ceremony comparable to and presumably derived from the Algonquian Midewiwin. It is impossible to determine if this bean was the mescalbean or to what Dakota bands Riggs was referring in his account. However, this description probably pertains to Eastern Dakota bands since Riggs states that the ceremony was largely confined to the Eastern Dakota and he worked almost exclusively with the Santee, an Eastern Dakota group. This inconclusive bit of data provides the only published information regarding the possible use of mescalbeans by the Sioux. Howard (n.d.) reports that the Brule attached mescalbeans to their buckskin shirts, leggings, and dresses; I have reproduced in Figure 22 a photograph of a Brule man wearing a string of mescalbeans as a hair ornament (National Anthropological Archives, Smithsonian Institution, negative number 15805). Contemporary Yankton individuals attach mescalbeans to their buckskin dresses, and mescalbean bandoleers are worn in the Yankton peyote ceremony (Howard n.d.).

Specimen 75: <u>Man's tanned and fringed buckskin shirt</u>; 152.5 cm wide across the back, from sleeve tip to sleeve tip; 60.0 cm across the back from shoulder to shoulder; 79.0 cm long on the back side; 73.5 cm long on the front side. The shirt is made of a single piece of leather, with a head hole cut out in the center. The front and back sides are joined with leather fringe ties. The bottom of the shirt and sleeves are cut into short, square fringes. Two panels of porcupine quill embroidery pass over the shoulders of the shirt, embellishing both the front and back sides. Similar panels are found on the back sides of the sleeves. The porcupine quill panels carry a design composed of a series of violet stars with white centers separated by a series of red and white horizontal lines with violet triangles extending from them. Strips of very long, tanned buckskin fringe are attached to the shirt underneath these panels, and ten mescalbeans are attached to this fringe on each side of the back of the shirt at the point where the embroidered panel on the back of the shirt joins the one on the sleeve. In addition, six mescalbeans are located about a third of the way down each sleeve on the back side. No mescalbeans are attached to the front of the shirt. This specimen bears a total of thirty-two mescalbeans. The seeds range in color from brownish-red to scarlet rather than the maroon color that often characterizes mescalbeans used for such purposes. The seeds have been perforated by burning; all are of medium size, ranging from 1.2 to 1.7 cm in length and 1.0 to 1.3 cm in width.

Smithsonian Institution, catalogue number 357510, accession number 113605. No collection locality or date given. Acquired by bequest from the Estate of Victor J. Evans. Accession date: March 25, 1931.

Specimen 76: <u>Woman's dress</u>; no measurements were made of this specimen. This elaborately decorated dress is heavily beaded across the top from the midpoint of each sleeve to the midpoint of the other, front and back, from the neck to the bust. A large white shell disk is attached at the neck of the front of the dress, but none appears on the reverse side in this location. The beads are arranged in geometrical designs on a white background. Below the beaded portion on each side of each sleeve is a row of four small shell disks followed by another row of beads, then a row of shells. The ends and bottom edges of the sleeves are fringed as is the bottom of the dress. Below the beaded section across the top of the dress, front and back, is a row of four large shell disks between which are looped buckskin thongs. A string of small glass trade beads is wrapped around these thongs where they emerge from the dress. Spherical and tubular glass beads, mescalbeans and shells are strung on these thongs. At about the waist level, front and back, is located another row of beaded geometrical designs on a white background. Just below the midpoint of the dress is looped another series of buckskin thongs, also wrapped at their base with strings of small glass beads and also bearing spherical and tubular glass beads, mescalbeans, and shells. On the front side of the dress, these thongs are looped between a series of small shell disks arranged in three rows; the disks in each of the rows are progressively smaller than those in the previous row. No disks are found on the back of the dress. Just above the bottom fringe of the dress is a row of shells followed by a row of small white shell disks, then two more rows of shells, and finally a row of beads. No measurements or counts of the mescalbeans on this specimen were made.

Dayton Museum of Natural History, catalogue number A-2571, accession number 3573. Collected by H. E. Talbott in 1875. No collection locality is given, but the accompanying catalogue information indicates that this dress belonged to "Shovel Foot."

Figure 23a. Specimen 77: A Sioux bear claw necklace with mescalbean spacers. Smithsonian Institution, catalogue number 361872.

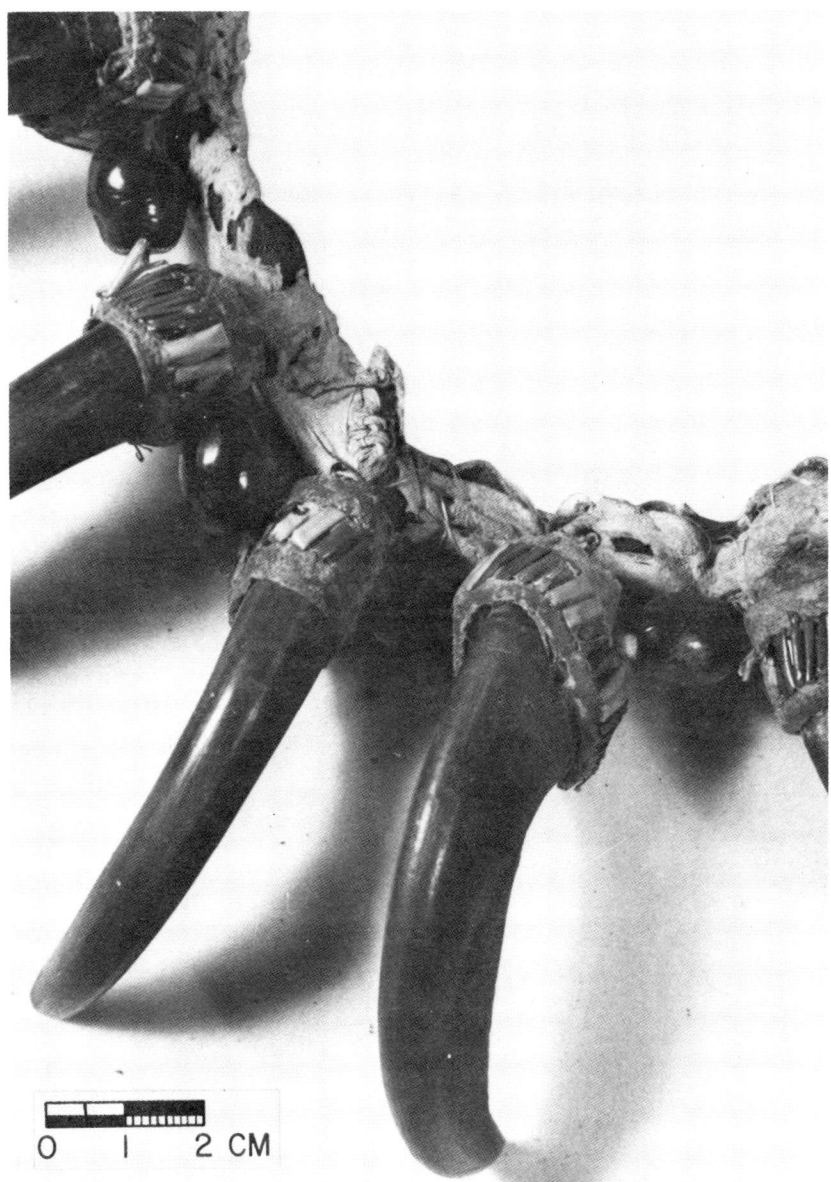

Figure 23b. An enlarged view of the same specimen.

Specimen 77: <u>Bear claw necklace</u> (Fig. 23), 133 cm long. A tanned leather strip is sewn around a strip of cloth to form the base of this necklace. The leather strip extends beyond the cloth at each end of the necklace for tying. The bear claws perhaps are imitation, made from horn, and each claw is wrapped at its base with a rawhide strip decorated with porcupine quills dyed red and yellowish orange. Each claw is perforated at its base and attached to the cloth-leather strip by a rawhide string. The string loops through the claw and the cloth-leather strip, passes back through the claw and then through a mescalbean spacer. There are a total of twenty-seven claws, separated by twenty-one mescalbeans. There are spaces for twenty-six mescalbean spacers, five of which apparently have been lost. The mescalbeans are all of the same deep maroon color and range in size from 1.5 to 2.0 cm long and 1.0 to 1.5 cm wide.

Smithsonian Institution, catalogue number 361872, accession number 113605. No collection date or locality given. Acquired by bequest from the Estate of Victor J. Evans. Accession date: March 26, 1931.

Specimen 78: <u>Cradle</u>, consisting of two wooden foundation boards decorated with a yellow ribbon and brass tacks at the top and a container for the child (referred to here as the "cradle proper"), fully beaded on the exterior and lined with cotton cloth on the interior. The wooden frame is 126 cm long, 35.5 cm wide at the top, and 13 cm wide at the bottom. The cradle proper is 86 cm long, 28 cm wide at the top, and 26 cm wide at the bottom before it tapers to a point. The two halves of the cradle proper are joined by buckskin ties. Inside is a baby's white bonnet and a diaper-sheet made of several pieces of feed-sack cloth sewn together. The cloth bears the trademark of "Weatherford ML'G Co". The exterior of the cradle proper is beaded with black, red, light blue, yellow, green, and pink trade beads in geometric designs on a white beaded background. The geometric designs are arranged in six rows along the sides and back of the cradle. At the middle of each of these rows of designs on each side of the cradle are attached several ribbons (red or yellow in color) and mescalbeans, faceted blue glass beads, and metal (brass?) bells strung on tanned leather strings. Originally two such strings seem to have been attached to each design on each side of the cradle and there are places for eleven sets of strings and ribbons; however, some strings have fallen off the cradle and apparently have been lost. The pattern of the beads, mescalbeans and bells on the leather strings is as follows: a blue bead appears first, followed by a mescalbean, then alternating blue beads and mescalbeans to the end of the string where a bell is attached. Most complete strings have a total of five blue beads, five mescalbeans, and one bell, but some have four blue beads and four mescalbeans while others have six of each. A total of eighty-five mescalbeans are present on this specimen. All are maroon and seem to have been perforated with a hot drill. They are small to medium in size, ranging from 1.0 to 1.5 cm in length and 0.8 to 1.1 cm in width.

Smithsonian Institution, catalogue number 358176, accession number 113605. No collection date or location given. Acquired by bequest from the Estate of Victor J. Evans. Accession date: March 26, 1931.

Specimen 79: <u>Feather headdress</u>, 220 cm long. A brimless felt hat forms the base of this headdress, to which are attached two red felt streamers. Eagle feathers, wrapped at the base with red cloth and tipped with pink feathers and yellow, red, pink, and brown dyed horsehair, are attched to the base and streamers of the headdress. A beaded band of blue and white triangles is sewn along the forehead of the headdress; at both ends of it are attached a white feather and a leather reptilian figure. The reptilian figure on the wearer's right is decorated with red, white, yellow, green, and blue trade beads while the figure on the left is decorated in blue and white beads. Also at the termination of the forehead band on either side are leather strings with blue, green, and yellow glass beads and metal tubular beads attached. One long string of mescalbeans forms a double row across the front of the headdress above the beaded band and falls down in a loop on either side. At the lowest point of the loop on both sides is attached a feather (blue on the left side and white on the right) cut so that only the tip remains. Also, a green cotton cord is attached to the bottom of the loop on the right side. This specimen bears a total of one hundred ninety-three mescalbeans all of which have been perforated with a hot drill. They vary in color from dark to light maroon. Most are rather large but smaller mescalbeans are present on the right side of the string. They range in size from 1.0 to 1.7 cm long and 0.7 to 1.2 cm wide.

Smithsonian Institution, catalogue number 357478, accession number 113605. No collection date or locality given. Acquired by bequest from the Estate of Victor J. Evans. Accession date: March 26, 1931.

Specimen 80: <u>Teton Dakota man's buckskin shirt</u> with very small mescalbeans attached. This specimen was collected from the Teton Dakota by M. G. Chandler and placed on loan in the collections of the Museum of Anthropology, University of Michigan, from 1929 to 1938. It was examined by Volney H. Jones on September 2, 1935. A more detailed description of it is not available at present.

Specimen 81: <u>Oglala Sioux mescalbean necklace</u> with a <u>Sophora secundiflora</u> pod attached; 61 cm long doubled, approximately 128 to 130 cm long when stretched out into a single strand. The specimen consists of ninety-nine mescalbeans strung on two commercial cotton strings. The string is joined almost at its ends by a rawhide string that also serves to attach a two-seeded <u>Sophora secundiflora</u> pod to the necklace. The pod is perforated in the center of both sides of each seed and a black line is drawn around the pod just to the exterior of the perforations. According to the catalogue information accompanying this specimen, the pod was employed as a rattle. The two ends of the necklace extend below the pod and bear eight mescalbeans each. Each end of the string is knotted below the last mescalbean. The mescalbeans are much lighter in color than those usually encountered on such specimens, varying from tannish- to brownish-red. All apparently have been perforated with a hot drill. The majority of the seeds are uniformly medium in size; they range from 1.2 to 1.6 cm in length to approximately 1.0 to 1.1 cm in width.

Museum of the American Indian (Heye Foundation), catalogue number 14/5703. No collection date or locality given. Presented by Mrs. Margaret Gilbert. Accession date: 1926.

Specimen 82: Upper Yanktonai buckskin leggings with mescalbeans attached to the flaps. This specimen has been examined by Howard (n.d.) who feels that the style of the leggings suggests a Southern rather than Northern Plains provenience.

North Dakota State Historical Museum. No catalogue information obtained. Specimen reportedly was collected among the Upper Yanktonai of Ft. Yates, North Dakota.

Tonkawa

Gatschet (1884:82) reports that mescalbeans were consumed by both men and women during the performance of the Tonkawa Deer Dance. The Tonkawa also may have employed mescalbeans therapeutically (Whitebread 1925:21; see the Tonkawa specimen described below). More recently, Howard (1957:84) learned from Ponca and Omaha informants that Tonkawa individuals in the early twentieth century performed mescalbean ceremonies and, during their peyote meetings, consumed an apparently intoxicating tea prepared from both mescalbeans and peyote.

Specimen 83: Mescalbeans, collected by Dr. Henry McElderry, an Army doctor assigned to Ft. Griffin in Schackelford County, Texas, probably in 1868 from Tonkawas who were residing near the fort. The following information was associated with these mescalbeans: "OUWAH-CHALUC. The seeds of Sophora speciosa Bente. [a synonym of Sophora secundiflora], a shrub or small tree growing in Texas. Contains a poisonous alkaloid. Used as medicine by the Tonkawas. The Indians are said to use them occasionally as an intoxicant, half a bean producing delirious exhiliration followed by a long period of sleep" (Charles Whitebread 1941: letter to Volney H. Jones, January 9, 1941).

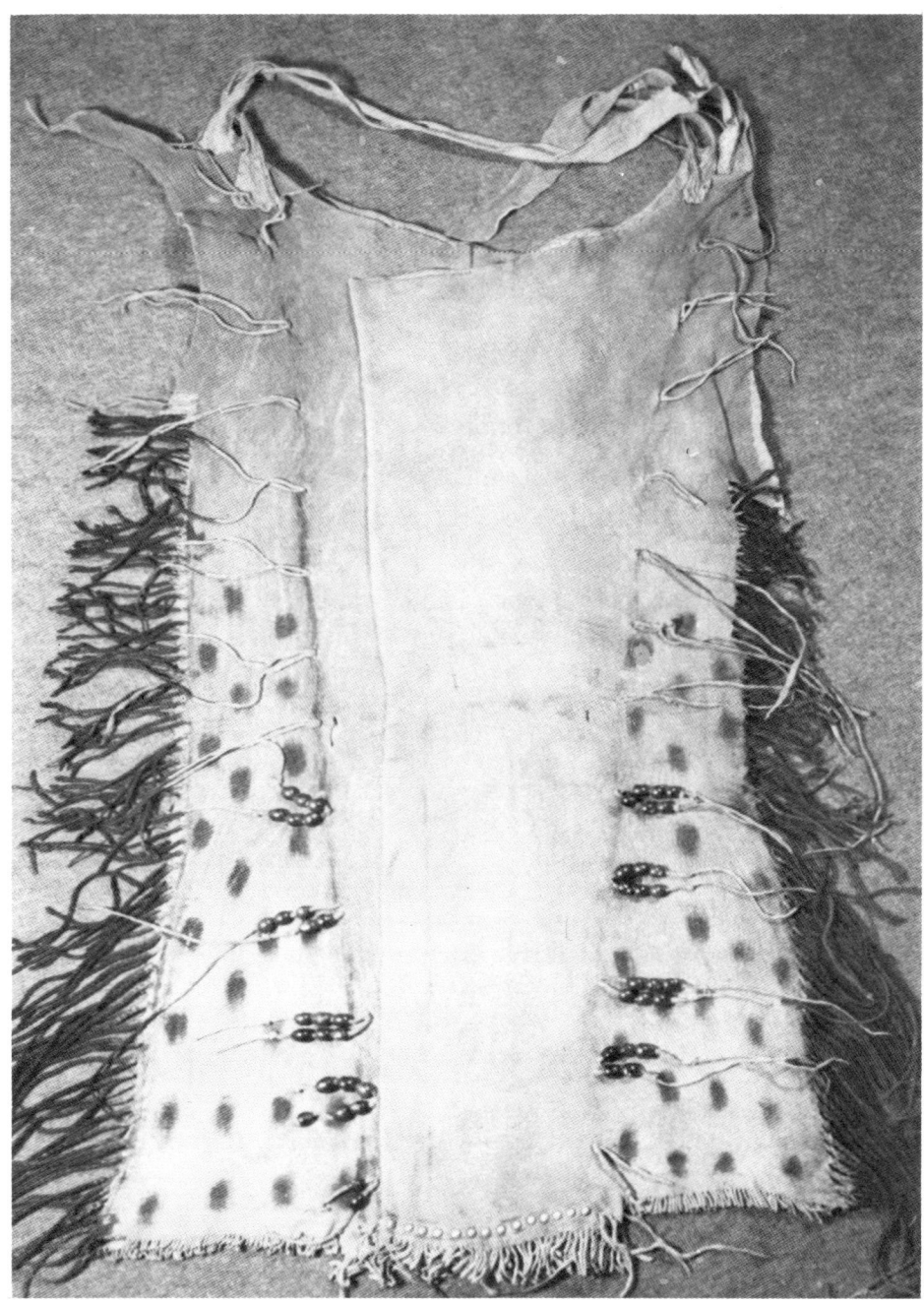

Figure 24. Specimen 84: A pair of Wichita leggings with mescalbeans attached to leather thongs looped through the sides of the leggings. University Museum, University of Pennsylvania, catalogue number L-84-1839 a-b.

Smithsonian Institution, catalogue number 53436. According to William K. Jones (1969:73), these mescalbeans were lost when the McElderry collection was transferred from the Army Medical Museum to the Smithsonian Institution in 1869.

Wichita

Several Wichita groups are reported to have consumed an emetic and purgative decoction of mescalbeans during the celebration of their first fruits ceremonies (Berlandier 1969:94-95, 143-44; Terán 1870:266). In addition, initiates of the Wichita Deer Dance are said to have ingested from one to several mescalbeans to induce an unconscious state accompanied by visions (Dorsey 1902:235-39, 1904:16-17). More recently, Schultes (1937:145) relates that Wichita individuals used to eat a single mescalbean apiece before engaging in footraces "to prevent panting afterwards."

Specimen 84: Man's tanned and fringed buckskin leggings (Fig. 24), 78 cm long at longest point (including fringe), 33 cm wide at both top and bottom (excluding fringe), and 50 cm wide at bottom including fringe. A series of buckskin thongs are looped through the leggings to taper them; each thong has two loose ends. The bottoms of the leggings are cut into short, squarish fringes. Longer fringes, dyed a dark blue-green, are attached to the sides of the leggings. The leggings are stained a yellowish-brown color with a series of alternating, parallel vertical green and red lines drawn on the major portion of the leggings to the interior of the buckskin thongs starting about midway. A number of dark blue-green dots are drawn between the thongs and the side fringes. Metal brads line the edges of the leggings to the interior of the side fringe, on the side of the leggings opposite the one that bears the loose ends of the tapering strings; these metal brads also are located along the bottom of the leggings on the sides where the loose ends of the tapering strings are present. Mescalbeans are attached to some of the loose ends of these strings. No mescalbeans are attached to the first seven pairs of these strings (from the top). On the right legging three mescalbeans are strung on each end of the next four pairs of strings, except the last end of the last string where two mescalbeans are attached, making a total of twenty-three mescalbeans on the right legging. On the left legging, there are seven ends with three mescalbeans each, one end with two mescalbeans, and two ends with one mescalbean each, or a total of twenty-five mescalbeans on the left legging. Metal clips sometimes are attached to the strings below the mescalbeans. All of the forty-eight mescalbeans attached to this specimen are a deep maroon color and all are of generally the same size, ranging from 1.0 to 1.5 cm long and 0.8 to 1.1 cm wide. They apparently have been perforated with a hot drill, but some of the seeds do not display the discoloration usually associated with this method of perforation.

University Museum, University of Pennsylvania, catalogue number L-84-1839a - b. Collected by A. H. Gottschall apparently in Sugar Creek, Oklahoma. No collection date given; the Academy of Natural Sciences of Philadelphia received it in May, 1914. Lent by the Academy of Natural Sciences in 1937.

Specimen 85: <u>Medicine string</u>, 104 cm long (when stretched out into a single strand). This specimen is composed of three strands of buffalo hair rope and one string of seed beads strung on a buckskin thong. The strands of buffalo hair and seed beads are joined at four points. At the upper point, a tuft of buffalo wool and a stone projectile point are attached to the string by means of a rawhide string. Tufts of buffalo wool also appear at the side points where the various strands are tied together. The buffalo hair strands are knotted at the bottom of the string and their loose ends hang down below. A bunch of buffalo wool also is tied to the string at this point. The two ends of the string of seed beads also dangle below the point where the buffalo hair strands are knotted together. I have identified the seed beads making up this necklace as eighty-eight <u>Sophora secundiflora</u> seeds and one <u>Erythrina flabelliformis</u> seed. All the seeds have been perforated with a hot drill and most are wrinkled and cracked. The mescalbeans vary a great deal in color, ranging from tannish- to brownish-red, and they also vary somewhat in size, from 1.0 to 1.7 cm in length and from 0.8 to 1.3 cm in width. The <u>E. flabelliformis</u> seed is reddish brown and 1.4 cm long by 0.9 cm wide.

American Museum of Natural History, catalogue number 50.1/6364, accession number 1911-46. Collected by P. E. Goddard, apparently in Oklahoma in 1911. Accession date: 1911.

Specimen 86: <u>Mescalbean necklace or bandoleer</u> with "fetish doll" attached. This specimen consists of one hundred and twenty-one mescalbeans, perforated with a hot drill and strung on commercial black cotton cord. The two ends of the string are joined by passing through a large, light blue bead with white curlicue designs on its surface. Mescalbeans are strung on the two loose ends of the string below this bead (four mescalbeans on one end, five on the other), below which two metal clasps are attached to each end. Each clasp bears a large marbled glass bead, three reddish in color, a fourth translucent wiht gold marbling. A metal bell is attached below one red bead on each end of the necklace. A buckskin figure of a man is attached to the necklace on the wearer's right at about neck level. The figure bears rows of trade beads around his neck, his waist, and along the edges of his shirt and leggings. A silver pendant hangs around his neck and silver chains serve as ear ornaments. According to the exhibit information accompanying this specimen (in 1946), this figure is "supposed to bring good fortune." The majority of the mescalbeans are of a generally uniform deep maroon color though some are slightly lighter. The seeds vary considerably in size, ranging from 0.9 to 1.7 cm in length and 0.7 to 1.4 cm in width. The specimen as a whole is 73 cm long when doubled and approximately 149 cm long when stretched out into a single strand.

Museum of the American Indian (Heye Foundation), catalogue number 2/1704. Collected by M. R. Harrington in Oklahoma, circa 1909. Accession date: 1909.

Winnebago

Available evidence indicates that the Winnebago did not employ mescalbeans prior to their adoption of the Peyote Religion and that their subsequent use of them has been exclusively for seed beads in association with peyote paraphernalia. I have not personally examined any of the Winnebago specimens described here. Information on these specimens was supplied by Volney H. Jones and the Wisconsin Historical Society.

Specimen 87: Two mescalbean necklaces, formerly owned by John Rave, a prominent leader of the Peyote Church in the late nineteenth and early twentieth centuries. The smaller of these two necklaces consists of fifty-six mescalbeans strung on a rawhide thong. The larger and more elaborate necklace is composed of sixty-nine mescalbeans strung on what is apparently commercial cotton cord. In addition, glass beads are strung on the cord at intervals (usually after a group of seven mescalbeans) and eight evenly spaced shells are attached to the necklace by rawhide strings. According to the accompanying catalogue information, "Mr R[ave] states that the sea shells in the necklace signify that the wearer is possessed of universal knowledge, his knowledge extending even to the depths of the water. He possesses the intelligence of even the water animals." Mr. Rave is reported to have received these necklaces as a gift from a Mr. John White, a leader of the (Winnebago ?) Peyote Church, when Mr. Rave joined.

Wisconsin State Historical Society, catalogue numbers 1954.1887 and 1954.1888. Collected from Mr. Rave apparently in 1911 when he was visiting in Wisconsin from his home in Nebraska with local members of the Peyote Church. Accession date: August 3, 1911.

Specimen 88: "Sacred mescal bean necklace" worn in Peyote ceremonies: approximately 164 cm in circumference. Eagle claws, one bone, and two horn pendants are attached to the necklace.

Wisconsin State Historical Society, catalogue number 1956.8341. Collected in 1920 from Winnebago at Black River Falls, Wisconsin. Originally a part of the Rahr Collection of Manitowoc, Wisconsin, this necklace was purchased by the Wisconsin State Historical Society from the Albert G. Heath Collection, Logan Museum, Beloit College, Beloit, Wisconsin. Accession date: March, 1956.

Specimen 89: Mescalbean necklace worn in peyote ceremonies; approximately 120 cm in circumference. Two carved bone pendants are attached to the necklace.

Wisconsin State Historical Society, catalogue number 1956.8373. Collected from Walter St. Cyr of Wisconsin. No collection date or specific locality given. Purchased by the Wisconsin State Historical Society from the Albert G. Heath Collection, Logan Museum, Beloit College, Beloit, Wisconsin. Accession date: March, 1956.

Specimen 90: Peyote whistle, made from an eagle wingbone. A triangular air hole is cut into the top of the whistle. This hole is converted into a representation of a tipi by the incision of three short lines at its apex to represent lodgepoles. Above this tipi are three more representations: the sun, a crescent moon, and a five-pointed star with beams of light radiating from it. The end of the whistle opposite the air hole is perforated. A rawhide string passes through this perforation. A small perforated claw and a mescalbean are strung on this string.

Wisconsin State Historical Society, catalogue number 1954.1884. Purchased from Oliver Lemere of Madison, Wisconsin. Accession date: September 5, 1929.

Specimen 91: A single mescalbean collected from the Winnebago by Mr. Thomas R. Roddy. Mescalbeans apparently have been employed only as items of paraphernalia in the Winnebago Peyote ceremonies since Mr. Roddy states emphatically (in Blair 1912, vol. 2:281) that the Winnebago never consumed mescalbeans.

Wisconsin State Historical Society, catalogue number E488, accession number 3357. Donated by Miss Emma H. Blair of Madison, Wisconsin.

Unidentified

Specimen 92: Deertail fan or wand, 39 cm long. This specimen consists of several white portions of deer tails topped with the black tip of a deer tail, all of which are attached to a stick to give the impression of one very large deer tail. The grip of this fan is wrapped with tan cloth with red streaks and a string of small white trade beads. A rawhide string is wrapped around the stick at the top of the grip. Six Sophora secundiflora seeds are strung on this string. Above this string is tied a cotton cord on which is strung a single Erythrina flabelliformis seed. At the bottom of the grip, one end of another rawhide string bearing two mescalbeans is tied to a strip of the cloth that is wrapped around the grip. The other end of the string is loose, extending 20.5 cm beyond where the mescalbeans are located. The mescalbeans vary in color from almost black through deep maroon to a brownish red. The mescalbeans located at the top of the grip vary in size from 1.0 to 1.3 cm in length and 0.7 to 1.0 cm in width. The two mescalbeans at the bottom of the grip measure 1.3 by 1.0 cm and 1.4 by 1.3 cm respectively. The single E. flabelliformis seed is a tannish-red color and measures 1.6 by 1.1 cm. Both the E. flabelliformis seeds and the mescalbeans have been perforated with a hot drill; the E. flabelliformis seed is cracked as a result.

American Museum of Natural History, catalogue number 50.2/6010. No collection or accession information available. The accompanying catalogue information suggests a Plains provenience for this specimen; it is almost identical with a Northern Cheyenne specimen described above (specimen 24).

Specimen 93: Two bracelets, consisting of the perforated seeds of Erythrina flabelliformis strung on cotton cord, which is knotted at each end. A tanned leather strip is tied to one end of each bracelet. Blue tubular trade beads are strung between the E. flabelliformis seeds and one red glass trade bead is strung on the end of one of the bracelets. A total of fourteen E. flabelliformis seeds are present, five on one bracelet, nine on the other. They are generally of the same color deep maroon to brown, and range in size from 1.0 to 1.6 cm long and 0.8 to 1.2 cm wide. They have been perforated with a hot drill; four of the seeds are cracked, because of either careless perforation or mishandling.

University Museum, University of Pennsylvania, catalogue number NA 3937. Collected in Oklahoma in 1913 by Mrs. P. H. Ray; no group affiliation of original owners given.

APPENDIX I.   INDEX OF SPECIMENS BY MUSEUM

<u>American Museum of Natural History</u>:   Northern Cheyenne #22; Comanche #30; Iowa #40; Kiowa #46; Omaha #57; Pawnee #65, 66, 67; Wichita #85; Unidentified #92.

<u>Arizona State Museum</u>, University of Arizona: Mescalero Apache #5; Western Apache #6; White Mountain Apache #7.

<u>Botanical Museum</u>, Harvard University: Kiowa #54.

<u>Dayton Museum of Natural History</u>:   Arapaho #10, 12, 13, 14; Crow #14; Sioux #76.

<u>Denver Art Museum</u>:   Kiowa #49, 50.

<u>Field Museum of Natural History</u>:   Northern Cheyenne #26; Kiowa #44; Pawnee #64.

<u>Florida State University Museum</u>:   Northern Cheyenne #23.

<u>Lowie Museum of Anthropology</u>, University of California at Berkeley: Kiowa #48; Osage #59; Santa Clara Tewa #59.

<u>Milwaukee Public Museum</u>:   Iowa #37, 38.

<u>Museum of the American Indian</u>, Heye Foundation: Chiricahua Apache #4; Comanche #29, 32, 33, 34, 35; Iowa #39, 41; Kickapoo #42; Missouri #56; Omaha #58; Oto #60, 61, 62, 63; Sac and Fox #69, 70, 71, 72, 73; Oglala #81; Wichita #86.

<u>Museum of the Plains Indian</u>:   Cheyenne #19.

<u>National Museum of Natural History</u>, Smithsonian Institution: Arapaho #8; Cheyenne #15, 16, 17, 18; Southern Cheyenne #28; Comanche #36; Kiowa #43, 51, 55; Ponca #68; Shoshone #74; Sioux #75, 77, 78, 79; Tonkawa #83; Wichita #36.

<u>North Dakota State Historical Museum</u>:   Upper Yanktonai #82.

<u>Peabody Museum of Archaeology and Ethnology</u>, Harvard University: Northern Cheyenne #21; Crow #21; Kiowa #45, 52.

Appendix I, continued

Peabody Museum of Natural History, Yale University: Northern Cheyenne #24, 25, 27.

Texas Archeological Research Laboratory, University of Texas at Austin: Prehistoric Southwestern Texas #2.

Texas Tech University Museum: Prehistoric Southwestern Texas #1.

University Museum, University of Pennsylvania: Apache #3; Arapaho #9, 11; Comanche #31; Kiowa #53; Wichita #84; Unidentified #93.

Western Frontier Museum, Philmont Scout Ranch: Kiowa #47.

Wisconsin State Historical Society: Winnebago #87, 88, 89, 90, 91.

LITERATURE CITED

Adovasio, J. M. and G. F. Fry

   1976 Prehistoric psychotropic drug use in Northeastern Mexico and Trans-Pecos Texas. Economic Botany 30:94-96.

Berlandier, Jean L.

   1969 The Indians of Texas in 1830, edited by John C. Ewers and translated by Patricia R. Leclercq. Washington: Smithsonian Institution Press.

Blair, Emma H., ed. and trans.

   1911-1912 The Indian tribes of the upper Mississippi Valley and region of the Great Lakes. 2 vols. Cleveland: The Arthur H. Clark Company.

Butler, Charles T., Jr.

   1948 A West Texas rock shelter, unpublished MA thesis. Department of Anthropology, University of Texas, Austin, Texas.

Campbell, T. N.

   1958 Origin of the mescal bean cult. American Anthropologist 60:156-60.

Castetter, Edward F., and M. E. Opler

   1936 The ethnobiology of the Chiricahua and Mescalero Apache. University of New Mexico Bulletin, Biological Series, vol. 4, no. 5.

Churchill, George W.

    1946   Dance of triumph. Collier's 117:22-23.

Clark, William P.

    1885   The Indian sign language. Philadelphia: L. R. Hamersly & Company.

Densmore, Frances

    1922   Northern Ute music. Smithsonian Institution, Bureau of American Ethnology Bulletin 75.

    1929   Pawnee music. Smithsonian Institution, Bureau of American Ethnology Bulletin 93.

Dorsey, George A.

    1902   Wichita tales. I. Origin. Journal of American Folk-Lore 15:215-39.

    1904   The mythology of the Wichita. Carnegie Institution of Washington Publication No. 21.

Dorsey, J. Owen

    1884   Omaha sociology. Smithsonian Institution, Bureau of Ethnology Annual Report 3:205-370.

    1894   A study of Siouan cults. Smithsonian Institution, Bureau of Ethnology Annual Report 11:351-544.

Ewers, John C.

    1945   Blackfeet crafts. Department of the Interior, United States Indian Service, Education Division, Indian Handcraft Pamphlet No. 9.

Ford, Richard I.

    1972   Barter, gift, or violence: an analysis of Tewa intertribal exchange, in Social exchange and interaction, edited by Edwin N. Wilmsen. Museum of Anthropology, University of Michigan, Anthropological Paper No. 46, pp. 21-45.

García, Fr. Bartholomé

    1760   Manual para adminstrar los santos sacramentos. . . México.

Gatschet, Albert S.

    1884   Tonkawe language, collected at Fort Griffin, Shackleford Co., Texas in Sept. - Oct. 1884, unpublished manuscript. Smithsonian Institution, National Anthropological Archives, ms. 1008.

Ghosal, S., and S. K. Dutta

    1971   Alkaloids of *Abrus precatorius*. Phytochemistry 10:195-98.

Gilmore, Melvin R.

    1919   Uses of plants by the Indians of the Missouri River region. Smithsonian Institution, Bureau of American Ethnology Annual Report 33:43-154.

    1924   Teoka[n]ha's sacred bundle. Museum of the American Indian, Heye Foundation. Indian Notes 1:52-62.

Harrington, M. R.

    1913   A visit to the Otoe Indians. University of Pennsylvania, The Museum Journal 4:107-13.

    1914   Sacred bundles of the Sac and Fox Indians. University of Pennsylvania, The University Museum, Anthropological Publications 4:121-262.

Hastings, James R., Raymond M. Turner, and Dougals K. Warren

    1972 An atlas of some plant distributions in the Sonoran Desert. The University of Arizona Institute of Atmospheric Physics, Technical Reports on the Meteorology and Climatology of Arid Regions No. 21.

Hatfield, G. M., L. J. J. Valdez, W. J. Keller, W. L. Merill, and V. H. Jones

    in press An investigation of <u>Sophora secundiflora</u> seeds (mescalbeans). Lloydia.

Holden, W. C.

    1937 Excavation of Murrah Cave. Texas Archeological and Paleontological Society Bulletin 9:48-73.

Howard, James H.

    n.d. Ritual uses of mescal and coral beans, unpublished manuscript in the possession of Volney H. Jones.

    1957 The mescal bean cult of the central and southern plains: an ancestor of the peyote cult? American Anthropologist 59:75-87.

    1960 Mescalism and peyotism once again. Plains Anthropologist 5:84-85.

    1962 Potawatomi mescalism and its relationship to the diffusion of the peyote cult. Plains Anthropologist 7:125-35.

    1965 The Ponca tribe. Smithsonian Institution, Bureau of American Ethnology Bulletin 195.

    1976 The Plains gourd dance as a revitalization movement. American Ethnologist 3:243-59.

James, Edwin

    1905   Account of an expedition from Pittsburgh to the Rocky Mountains, performed in the years 1819, 1820 in Early western travels 1748-1846, vols. 14-17, edited by Reuben G. Thwaites. Cleveland: The Arthur H. Clark Company.

Jones, David E.

    1972   Sanapia: Comanche medicine woman. New York: Holt, Rinehart and Winston.

Jones, Volney H., and William L. Merrill

    in press   Red Medicine: The mescalbean (Sophora secundiflora) among the Indians of North America, in Frontiers in ethnopsychopharmacology, edited by Jose Luis Diaz.

Jones, William K.

    1969   Notes on the history and material culture of the Tonkawa Indians. Smithsonian Institution, Smithsonian Contributions to Anthropology 2:65-81.

La Barre, Weston

    1957   Mescalism and peyotism. American Anthropologist 59:708-11.

    1969   The peyote cult. Enlarged edition. New York: Schocken Books.

    1972   The ghost dance: origins of religion. New York: Dell Publishing Company.

Lampe, Kenneth F., and Rune Fagerström

    1968   Plant toxicity and dermatitis: a manual for physicians. Baltimore: Williams and Wilkins Company.

Michigan Comission on Indian Affairs

    n.d.   The Indian in Michigan. n.p. [Lansing, Michigan].

Momaday, N. Scott

    1974   I am alive. . . *in* The world of the American Indian. Washington: National Geographic Society, pp. 10-27.

Murie, James R.

    1914   Pawnee Indian societies. Anthropological Papers of the American Museum of Natural History 11:543-644.

Opler, Morris E.

    1940   Myths and legends of the Lipan Apache Indians. Memoirs of the American Folk-Lore Society 36.

    1942   Myths and tales of the Chiricahua Apache Indians. Memoirs of the American Folk-lore Society 37.

Parsons, Elsie C.

    1941   Notes on the Caddo. Memoirs of the American Anthropological Association 57.

Powers, William K.

    1972   Indians of the southern Plains. New York: Capricorn Books.

Riggs, Stephen R.

    1893   Dakota grammar, texts, and ethnography. Department of the Interior, U.S. Geographical and Geological Survey of the Rocky Mountain Region, Contributions to North American Ethnology 9.

Robbins, Wilfred W., John P. Harrington, and Barbara Friere-Marreco

    1916   Ethnobotany of the Tewa Indians. Smithsonian Institution, Bureau of American Ethnology Bulletin 55.

Rudd, Velva E.

    1968   Legumionsae of Mexico--Faboideae. I. Sophoreae and Podalyrieae. Rhodora 70:492-532.

Schultes, Richard E.

    1937   Peyote and plants used in the peyote ceremony. Harvard University, Botanical Museum Leaflets 4:129-52.

Skinner, Alanson

    1915   Societies of the Iowa, Kansa, and Ponca Indians. Anthropological Papers of the American Museum of Natural History 11:679-802.

    1924-1927   The Mascoutens or Prairie Potawatomi Indians. Public Museum of the City of Milwaukee Bulletin 6:1-411.

    1927   Remarkable Oto necklace. Museum of the American Indian, Heye Foundation. Indian Notes 2:36-38.

    1926   Ethnology of the Ioway Indians. Public Museum of the City of Milwaukee Bulletin 5:181-354.

Smith, Ralph A.

    1961   The Comanche bridge between Oklahoma and Mexico, 1843-1844. Chronicles of Oklahoma 39:54-69.

    1962   Apache plunder trails southward, 1831-1840. New Mexico Historical Review 37:20-42.

Standley, Paul C.

    1928   Flora of the Panama Canal Zone. Contributions from the United States National Herbarium, vol. 27.

Stewart, Omer C.

    1974   Origin of the Peyote Religion in the United States. Plains Anthropologist 19:211-23.

Swanton, John R.

    1942   Source material on the history and ethnology of the Caddo Indians. Smithsonian Institution, Bureau of American Ethnology Bulletin 132.

Tanner, John

    1956   A narrative of the captivity and adventures of John Tanner. Original edition edited by Edwin James and published in New York in 1830. This edition introduced by Noel M. Loomis. Minneapolis: Ross & Haines, Inc.

Terán, Don Manuel de Mier y

    1870   Noticia de las tribus de salvajes conocidos que habitan en el Departamento de Tejas. Sociedad de Geografía y Estadística de la República Mexicana Boletín, segunda época 2:264-69.

Troike, Rudolph C.

    1962   The origins of plains mescalism. American Antrhopologist 64:946-63.

Voegelin, Erminie

    n.d.   Shawnee and Delaware fieldnotes, unpublished. Excerpts in the possession of Volney H. Jones.

Weltfish, Gene

    1937   Caddoan texts: Pawnee, south band dialect. Publications of the American Ethnological Society, vol. 17.

1965 The lost universe: the way of life of the Pawnee. New York: Ballantine Books.

Whitebread, Charles

1925 The Indian medical exhibit of the division of medicine in the United States National Museum. United States National Museum Proceedings 67:1-26.

Whitman, William

1937 The Oto. Columbia University Contributions to Anthropology 28.

1939 Xube, a Ponca autobiography. Journal of American Folk-Lore 52:180-93.

Woolsey, A. M.

1936 Excavation of a rockshelter on the Martin Kelly ranch, six miles southeast of Comstock in Val Verde County, Texas, February 13 to February 19, 1936, unpublished fieldnotes. Department of Anthropology, University of Texas, Austin, Texas.